EXPLORE YOURSELF
through ART

EXPLORE YOURSELF
through ART

VICKY BARBER

CARROLL & BROWN PUBLISHERS LIMITED

For my children James and Victoria
of whom I'm extremely proud.

First published in 2002 in the United Kingdom by:

Carroll & Brown Publishers Limited
20 Lonsdale Road
London NW6 6RD

Editor Kelly Thompson
Managing Art Editor Emily Cook
Photographer Jules Selmes
Indexer Madeline Weston

A CIP catalogue record for this book is available from the British Library.

ISBN 1–903258–44–8

Reproduced by Colourscan, Singapore
Printed by Graphicom, Italy

The activities and the information given within this book are in no way intended to replace the advice of a professional art therapist. Neither the author nor the publishers shall be liable or responsible for any loss, injury or damage allegedly arising from any information or suggestion in this book.

Contents

YOU inside

1

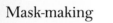

Foreword

I am proud and excited... to present you with this, one of the first visually practical guides to art therapy skills and techniques, which can be used and enjoyed by anyone, from complete novice to experienced artist.

This book includes step-by-step activities that allow you to experiment with colour, line, shape and texture in order to express your feelings honestly and spontaneously, to work through any problems or difficulties you may be experiencing, and, ultimately, to achieve greater self-knowledge.

I will lead you on a step-by-step creative journey and encourage you to start exploring and interpreting your own artwork for yourself to see what it can reveal to you. And you might even be lucky enough to discover hidden artistic talents along the way!

Making art therapy accessible to everyone has been one of my main goals since I realized just how effective a healing tool it can be. My experience of art therapy practice has shown me that the creative process of art can help promote emotional well-being in absolutely anyone who is willing

to try it. *The whole range of art techniques in the book—from Working with Clay, to Mask-making, to Assemblages—are tools that you can use to unleash the expression of your subconscious mind, bring problems closer to the surface, and even help you to resolve them.*

Creativity has been my anchor and focus all my life. I'm not sure where it came from as I didn't have a creative role model. All I know is that I have an insatiable appetite to express myself creatively and particularly like the challenge of making something out of nothing. I find it extremely satisfying, and indeed therapeutic, transforming a piece of paper into a bird, or an empty box into a house, for instance.

So it has always seemed natural for me to use my passion for art to encourage others. And when the opportunity arose for me to write this book, it was like a precious gift being given to me—an opportunity to share the magic of creativity and art therapy with as many people as possible.

Relax and enjoy the experience,

Vicky Barber, Art Therapist

The Artist Within You

Creativity is something innate in everyone, whoever you are, and wherever you come from. It is there for you to explore, develop, use and learn from at any time. And this book gives you the opportunity to do exactly that.

Everyone has the capacity to be creative. You don't have to be especially talented or gifted—it is always there within you waiting to burst out and possibly change your life. In fact, you are already an extremely creative person, whether you know it or not. Just look at some of the creative choices you make on a regular basis. For example, every morning when you get dressed you select your clothes based on colour, texture and shape. Similarly, decorating your home involves decisions about wall colour, the shape of the furniture and the texture of soft furnishings. These all involve the use of your artistic preferences and powers of creativity. It therefore seems a shame that we often shy away from exploring our creativity on a more conscious level.

SPONTANEITY OF YOUTH
When we were young, we had none of the creative inhibitions by which we are often limited as adults. We lived our lives with extreme enthusiasm and spontaneity, and therefore approached the world in

a heightened creative state. You have only to observe children at play to have confirmation of this: their creativity immediately takes over when presented with an object as simple as a cardboard box, transforming it into something fantastic—a rocket, a robot, a boat or even an animal—and injecting it with a life that fits into their fantasy world at the time.

LOST THE ARTIST WITHIN?

Maybe we are often less instinctively creative as adults due to fear of failure or looking stupid? After all, there is so much emphasis placed today on aesthetics that the finished appearance of an object often becomes more important than the process involved in its creation. This means that we start from a position of insecurity when making our own creations, a sense that we could never live up to our own, and others', aesthetic aspirations.

ACCESSING CREATIVITY

But it's never too late to rediscover the spontaneity

you had as a child—the ability to express how you are feeling with the stroke of a paintbrush, by making a collage, or creating a mask for yourself. *Explore Yourself Through Art* will guide you back to your lost world of creativity and help you to lead a rich, and enriching, creative life. And its beauty lies in the fact that it allows you to place the emphasis on the creative process and your exploration

of it, for a change, rather than the finished pieces of art themselves—so there is no pressure. And no specialist materials, prior knowledge or training are required: just you and the creativity within you!

Art Therapy and You

As far back as prehistoric times, art has been used as a form of communication and recreation, but art as a form of therapy and a tool of self-development is a much more recent phenomenon, which is gradually becoming accepted as a means of self-expression and self-exploration.

All projects in *Explore Yourself Through Art* are based on the principles and techniques of art therapy. This uses art as a medium to develop and enhance your creativity, thus raising your capacity for self-expression, self-awareness, self-comprehension, and, ultimately, self-confidence. Each project will lead you step by step through the creation of an object, and encourage you to question yourself on the creative process involved in making it, as well as on the finished piece that emerges.

WHO THE BOOK IS FOR

The activities are suitable and indeed beneficial for anyone interested in self-development. You are given the opportunity to focus on yourself, for a change, and the freedom to express yourself, your needs and your feelings in any way you like. However, the activities can be particularly useful tools for people who, for some reason, are hampered by a sense of frustration in life, for those who have difficulties expressing themselves verbally, or for individuals with specific problems that they feel they would like to resolve.

HOW TO USE THE BOOK

The first exercises you will meet are the warm-up ones (see pages 18–25), which introduce you to the four basic building blocks of art—colour, line, shape and texture. Then you can either choose to work through the main activities in the order

given; or select the activities most relevant to your mood, artistic preferences or emotional needs at the time. If the latter, refer to the *Aims* section at the top of each activity to check that it suits your purpose. Then put on your paint-shirt and begin. Use the list of questions at the end of each activity to explore the pieces you have created. Within each chapter there are also *Personal Insights* pages. These case studies provide further inspiration for interpreting your own work. Finally, the *Progressing Forward* section (see pages 156–7) will help you to establish what you have learned and gained from the experience, and what your next steps could be.

ADDITIONAL SUPPORT

It is a good idea to keep a diary to accompany you on your creative journey (see pages 14–15). You also may want to ask a good friend to become part of the process, to support you through the emotions that surface, and to celebrate your progress. Or, if you feel it is necessary, you might want to take it a step further and find an art therapist or counsellor to talk about your experiences and help you deal with any issues or problems that emerge. Because, although this is a self-help book, the information within it will only take you part of the way on your journey of self-discovery, and can't entirely replace on-site advice and interaction.

Art therapy over the years

Art as a form of therapy can be traced back to the early twentieth century. But it wasn't until the 1940s that art therapy became more widely practised, largely as a result of the work of figures such as Adrian Hill, who first used art as a form of personal recreation while convalescing from tuberculosis in a sanatorium. On discovering that it provided an outlet for the highly stressful impact of the Second World War, he started implementing it successfully among his fellow patients, too—seing art as a way of making connections with the psyche and expressing internal preoccupations. He went on to introduce art as an official form of therapy in many British hospitals and sanatoriums. It was then the social and political climate of the 1970s that moved art therapy into the realm of self-help, interactive groups. But it wasn't until the 1980s that it was accepted as a profession in its own right. Art therapy is now practised widely—within hospitals, day centres, schools and in private practice—for absolutely anyone who wants it.

Everything You Need

As well as sufficient creative space and time to carry out the projects in this book, you will need certain materials. Exactly what you require will depend on the particular project you tackle. There are, however, some basics worth acquiring so that you can be ready to create when the mood takes you.

The beauty of the activities in this book is that imagination and ingenuity are the keys; just about anything can be used to make your creations. However, we have included a list of materials at the top of each activity as a guideline for you. Generally it contains a mixture of essentials, plus some collage and recycled materials.

THE ESSENTIALS
You should gather together various sizes and colours of paper and card; drawing tools such as oil pastels, colouring pencils and felt-tip pens; paintbrushes and ready-mixed paints in black, white and primary colours; and various cutting and sticking implements; as well as some suitable clothes to work in. You can then pick and choose from this selection as you do each activity. It's a good idea to add to your basic kit as and when you have the money or the urge, as it will last for a long time if it is looked after properly.

COLLAGE MATERIALS
You also will want to collect some unusual items to help make your artistic creations

unique. Again, it's a good idea to collect these over time. At second-hand shops, garage sales, and fairs, look out for objects that catch your eye, such as interesting fabrics, wool and threads, sequins and buttons, little fun toys, or jewellery. You could even collect items when out walking in the park or on the beach, like fallen leaves, pebbles and shells. All such items may well come in useful.

RECYCLED MATERIALS

It is also fun to start collecting items from around the house that would otherwise be thrown out. In this way, you are helping the environment at the same time as gathering valuable creative material. Potential art objects can be as diverse as corks, sweet wrappers, tissue paper, straws, old packaging, photographs, newspapers, magazines, egg cartons and even old cardboard boxes—just anything that might be of use.

YOUR CREATIVE SPACE

Your creative space can be anywhere you feel appropriate—a spare room or simply an area in the kitchen, garage or dining room. It's best to find somewhere quiet so that you can give your full attention to the creative projects in hand. It's also important that you don't mind getting the area slightly messy. Otherwise, protect it with old sheets, newspapers or plastic covers. Keep cleaning materials and a few cloths and paper towels at hand just in case!

FINDING THE TIME

Try to set aside about an hour to complete any project in one sitting, so that your finished piece reflects your mood at the time. It's also advisable to start interpreting your artwork soon after creating it, as too much distance can dull the memory of the emotions experienced during the creative process.

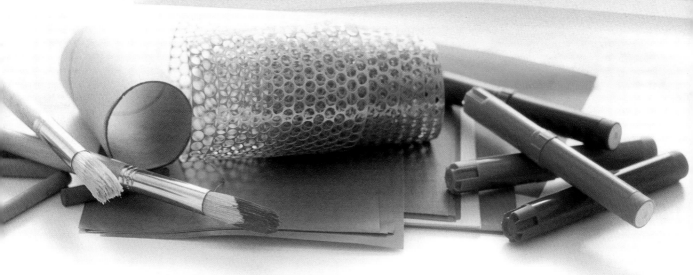

Your Therapy Diary

Art-making is a very personal experience, and the projects in this book are likely to result in significant emotional responses. It is important to keep a diary that allows you to record these experiences and gain insight from each activity.

Choose and buy a blank book that appeals to you. You will use this diary to externalize the many thoughts you have as you undertake the projects within this book. Such thoughts can be documented in both images and words. Whatever works best for you is fine. You should treat your diary as your constant companion and confidant—turning to it both during and after any project you undertake. This will enable you to deal with and learn from the feelings that emerge from each activity. Be sure to express and explore yourself as much as you want. The contents of your diary can be as messy as you like—write in it, draw in it and stick things in it—so that it becomes a living document and a work of art in itself. Place in it, too, any pictures, printed items, photographs or personal illustrations that may have particular significance. Then honor and treasure it as an extension of yourself.

WHAT TO INCLUDE?

Try not to underestimate the power of your own creativity and the ease with which it can challenge you by touching deeply buried places within yourself. Record in your diary any feelings, associations or memories you encounter during the creative process, whether positive or negative. Also write down your thoughts on and analyses of your finished creations and your possible reasons for making them. The list of questions at the end of each activity in the book provides a starting point for the type of questions you could ask yourself and try to answer honestly in your diary.

FAMOUS DIARIES

For inspiration, look to well-known historical figures, like the Mexican artist, Frida Kahlo, whose diary was painted in vivid colors, like her art—and encompassed love letters, political musings and bright paintings. Another example is Anne Frank, the Jewish girl who used her diary as a source of comfort and reflection while in hiding from the Nazi terrors of the Second World War.

Why keep a diary?

It is important to take time out from your projects to reflect on the emotions that the creative experiences have raised within you. Your creative diary is the perfect place for you to do this. It can supply you with:

an outlet for thoughts that arise during the creative process

•

the means to record how you feel about your finished artwork

•

a way of releasing and dealing with pent-up emotions

•

a private place to question yourself in ways you often don't

•

a trustworthy companion in which to confide

•

a lasting record of your changing emotional state

•

an effective tool to develop a deeper understanding of yourself

Doodle Book

As well as keeping a full diary to accompany your activities,

it is a good idea to start carrying a small book around

with you in which you can doodle and express yourself

creatively any time you feel the urge.

Have you you ever found yourself doodling while on the phone, or in a meeting? You probably have. Do you think there is a subconscious purpose behind it? Surely it provides you with a release for unspoken emotions and, as such, is a valuable means of spontaneous self-expression. After all, any personal externalization of your emotions, whether on a verbal or a visual level, tends to be meaningful and symbolic if looked into in more detail. It therefore seems a shame that

Doodling is simply a means of free and unrestrained, spontaneous self-expression. So whenever you feel like it, start doodling—whether it forms an actual image or not.

Having a fixed place in which to sketch and scribble whenever you feel the need—whether sitting in a café, travelling on a train or talking on the telephone, can be a useful resource. It is not meant specifically for use in conjunction with the activities within this book, but it can be:

•

an outlet to let your emotions run free at any given time

•

an extra means for you to become more in touch with your creative side, which, in turn, is likely to improve your expressive ability within the activities

•

a fixed place for you to preserve your expressive markings

•

a record of your spontaneous doodles, which could provide you with important insights into yourself if looked through and questioned from time to time

we usually end up scribbling on just any old scrap of paper, envelope or newspaper edge available, and simply throwing it away afterwards.

A VALUABLE RESOURCE

Buy a notebook or sketchpad that is small enough to slip into your pocket or handbag. Then, whenever you feel like doodling, simply take out this book and a pen or pencil, and draw or scribble whatever comes to your mind and flows from your hand. It is worth keeping your doodles together so that you can look back over them from time to time and see what striking features you notice in them.

Once you have started to fill your book with these insightful, creative gems, don't allow yourself to tear out pages just because you don't like them. Messiness is acceptable and is often a natural part of any creative process.

USING YOUR BOOK

Question yourself on why you might have drawn the doodles you have in order to see whether they reveal much about your character. Pay particular attention to any recurring doodles or ones that you think are particularly unusual.

EXPLORING **COLOUR**

Imagine what a dull world it would be without colour. Yet sometimes its effects are so subtle that we no longer even notice it around us. But the vast array of colours that we are exposed to on a daily basis plays a vital role in our well-being. So much so that colours are now integrated into our everyday expressions. For example, "He was feeling blue" is a universal description for feelings of sadness, and "She made him see red," signifies anger and danger. However, in addition to these generalizations, each of us tends also to have a personal colour-coding system, based on our own life experiences and cultures.

COLOUR EXERCISE

Think about a sentiment you want to depict, such as excitement or anger. Then choose a colour that will represent this for you, and use paint of this colour to cover a piece of white paper. Experiment with the depth of the colour using other paints or water, to lighten or darken it according to your mood. Use the same process with other emotions, too. Once your paintings are dry, tape them up on a wall to see how you feel about them. How did you find illustrating your emotions in terms of colours alone? Do you feel your chosen colours reflect your feelings accurately? If so, why? See right for examples of responses.

JANE: EXCITEMENT
Jane's feelings inspired her to use orange. She then used red and yellow to develop the colour so that it looked fiery and explosive, like her emotion.

Artists such as Mark Rothko and Yves Klein recognized the significance of personal responses to colour and are renowned for the striking use of it in their works. Rothko created large rectangles of bright colour within areas of background colour. He wanted to draw viewers into a full experience of colour and tone so that they could appreciate "the simple expression of the complex thought." Klein—most famous for his blue monochromes—wanted to explore the emotive qualities of colour and to inspire the viewer to move beyond the restrictions of preconceived meanings, allowing for a variety of interpretations.

To investigate your own associations with colours, try the exercise below. It explores how much impact colour has on you and will make you more confident using it to represent your feelings during the activities to come. Finally, it should stimulate your appreciation of colour, and elevate it to the importance it deserves.

NICK: CALM
Blue was Nick's colour of choice to represent calm. He then mixed in some white, pink and a touch of black to give it more depth, somewhat like a lake.

JOSIE: COMPANIONSHIP
When Josie thought of companionship, she painted varying tones of blazing yellow, with a few friendly, welcoming, abstract figures in the middle.

EXPLORING **LINE**

We are constantly making lines or marks on paper, yet we rarely stop to take much notice of them. However, spending a little time exploring and thinking about the lines you make, and the possible meaning behind them, can help you discover a lot about yourself and how you are generally feeling about life.

When we think of making a line, a straight line is usually what enters our minds first, but, of course, a line can develop in whatever direction you like. The direction you choose to make it travel, the intensity with which you draw it, and the size and

LINE EXERCISE

Think about a state of mind that you want to recreate—happiness or discontentment, for example. Then draw a line in any direction you want on paper, trying to capture this mood. Use any drawing implement—pen, pencil, felt-tip pen or paintbrush—to make your line(s) as thick or thin, light or heavy, and as short or long as you like. When your line is complete, go on to use the same process for other moods, and reflect on the end pieces. Why did you choose to draw the lines you did? Do they capture your feelings well? See right for examples of responses.

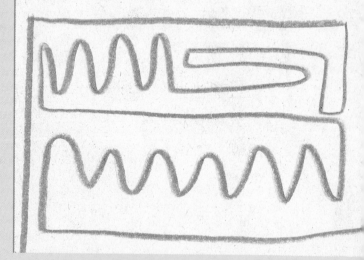

SARA: DISCONTENTMENT
A lack of contentment led Sara to create one long, changing line. She felt that the straight line showed her apathy and the jagged area reflected her anxiety.

shape you give it all can reveal a lot about your personality and how you feel at the time. An example of where lines are used to explore moods and personalities in detail is the art of graphology—the study of hand-writing.

However, line is also the basic language of most art, from a child's first drawing to works of famous artists. Vincent Van Gogh, for example, used different types of line to great effect in his paintings—from swirly, curved, light and wavy lines, to straight, parallel and heavy ones. Henri Matisse was well-known for his line drawings, too.

To investigate your own use of, attitude to, and associations with certain lines, try the exercise below. It also will help you to use line as a form of self-expression in itself, rather than always using it to draw a particular shape. This will, in turn, aid your visual-imaging skills within the activities in the main body of this book— something you might not be used to doing.

JUSTIN: FREEDOM
Justin used a thick, flowing line to depict freedom. The mix of straight and curved lines, and solid and broken paint show the variety this state provides.

EMILY: CONTENTMENT
To show contentment, Emily drew a relaxed, swirly line, incorporating lots of loops. The straight line on two sides reflected the stability she was feeling.

EXPLORING **SHAPE**

We live in a world entirely made up of shapes and forms, so it follows that our lives are greatly affected by them. Exploring the impact that various shapes have on you can help you to understand the reasons for many of your choices.

All sorts of shapes surround us on a daily basis— from natural cloud formations and landscape features, to the distinctive, man-made shapes of clothes, cars and buildings. And living in the image-conscious society that we do, we make daily decisions about form in purchases and judgments that we make. Visual forms often crop up in

SHAPE EXERCISE

Think about how you are feeling at present— energetic or lethargic, for example. Take a piece of paper and draw several variations of basic shapes— circles, squares or triangles—that might represent your mood. Then choose the one that best captures your feelings. Take another piece of paper and draw or paint your chosen shape in various sizes and formations on it. When you have finished, look at the pattern and see what words spring to mind. Go through the same process with other feelings and shapes. Compare the results of each and explore why you might have chosen the associations you did. Do you think that each page of shapes represents your chosen emotion? See right for examples of responses to this exercise.

KIRSTEN: RESPONSIBILITY
Squares and rectangles emerged when Kirsten depicted responsibility. She felt that boxes within boxes reflected her need to stay in control.

figures of speech, too. For example, someone who is "boxed in" can't escape a problem, a "circle of friends" describes a group of companions, and the phrase "eternal triangle" implies a complex relationship involving three people.

Shape and form, of course, always have been important in the art world, too. An Impressionist artist, Cézanne avoided classically arranged landscapes to such an extent that some said his landscapes had reduced nature to a few basic forms—the sphere, the cube, the pyramid and the cylinder. And Cubists, like Pablo Picasso and

Georges Braque, also experimented with abstract shapes and forms to break away from the conventions of the time. Their fragmented images rejected the traditional techniques of perspective, showing all points of view at once in order to explore underlying shape relationships.

To explore your own associations with various shapes, try the exercise below. This will help you to start thinking about shape and form, in preparation for using them to good effect within the main activities in this book.

DAVID: FREEDOM

Large, overlapping, circles came to mind when David thought of freedom. He painted bubble-like circles to remind him of fluidity, lightness and happiness.

MAX: ENERGY

To capture the essence of energy, Max used various triangles. To him, the many small, overlapping triangles evoke a sense of vitality and movement.

EXPLORING **TEXTURE**

Practically everything we come into contact with has a texture. Yet how often do we actually stop and appreciate these surfaces?

We experience textures from the moment we are born. In childhood, our curiosity leads us to explore textures by feeling all things new to us—our parent's skin and clothes, our various toys, water at bath-time, and so on. This process continues in adulthood each time we choose or buy an item as a result of how it feels—whether due to specific memories of that texture or more general associations with it. After all, textures can

TEXTURE EXERCISE

Identify a strong emotion or need that you are experiencing at present. Spend some time feeling various textures. Establish which of these could best capture the essence of your emotion. It could be anything—from velvet to sandpaper. Now go on to create an image to reflect your chosen texture(s): you could stick actual raw materials onto card, or you could use paints or magazine images to simulate your experience of the textures. When you have completed your creation, go through the same process for other emotions. Compare the resulting creations to one another, think about why you chose the materials you did, and decide whether you think they accurately represent each feeling. See right for some examples of responses to this exercise.

SIMON: SECURITY
A need to feel safe led Simon to arrange a mixture of soft-feeling fabrics—from fake fur, to feathers, to thread—that reminded him of his home comforts.

be sensuous and emotive, ranging from soft silk or cool marble, to rough pebble dash or sandpaper. Texture therefore plays quite a substantial role in our lives.

Artists during the Pop Art period of the 1950s and 1960s were particularly fascinated with the use of textures. Jackson Pollock's paintings were textured by the sheer volume of paint he applied to the canvas during his action-painting phase, which gives his paintings an element of instability and excitement. Claes Oldenburg also used textures to great effect in his art. One of his most

famous sculptures, *Soft Fur Good Humors* (1963)— a model of four ice lollies made of different fur fabrics, with a bite taken out of each—perfectly illustrates his ingenious use of materials that were full of surprises and inventive in themselves.

The exercise below allows you to experiment with textures to discover what your own associations and preferences are. It should allow you to become more in touch with your textural associations, and to explore how you can use them to express and reflect your feelings within the main projects in this book.

VALERIE: ANGER
To depict anger, Valerie chose to scrunch up large pieces of paper and netting, paint the card green and attach it all together with drawing pins.

PATRICIA: JOY
Great happiness inspired Patricia to piece together lots of small, unusual-feeling objects, including tiny beads and sequins, on a smooth surface.

INTERPRETING YOUR WORK

It is important to think about your creative process and finished artwork at the end of every activity in order to get the most out of the projects. The ability to explore and interpret your creations is, after all, a crucial part of the therapeutic experience offered in this book.

Too often we look to other people to evaluate our own creativity. But as other people's preferences are often very different to our own, their opinions can not only be inaccurate but also upset us. The interpretations of the images beneath show how differently people can respond to the same stimulus. The key to and beauty of art in the context of art therapy is that it isn't important what others think. It's what you think that matters—your ideas and your interpretations. After all, the activities in this book aim to promote self-awareness and self-development. You are under no pressure, as there are no right or wrong answers—just lots of possible ones, all stemming from you.

The artwork you make contains numerous clues as to your thoughts—both conscious and subconscious—as you made it. Your creation is like a house that you are about to enter. The first

DIFFERENT INTERPRETATIONS

JANE'S
The green swirls evoked feelings of happiness and security at being surrounded by powerful, all-embracing Mother nature.

NICK'S
This image brought up feelings of frustration and constriction within him—a desire for the passion within him to escape outside the rough black outline.

NICOLA'S
The large, confident, sweeping nature of this painting symbolized freedom in art and in life for Nicola— a reflection of how she would like to live life.

and bravest step is to enter the house at all. Then, you are faced with many rooms to explore, each with lots of dimensions due to choices that the decorator has made. But it is up to you which choices you think about in more detail in order to learn about the decorator and his or her tastes. Similarly, your use of certain colours, lines, shapes or textures in an artistic creation can reveal a lot about you and your feelings when examined.

At the end of every activity in this book there are questions that act as a starting point for your exploration of what you created and why. Lay out or hang up your creation(s), observe it/them for a short time, and use these questions as a starting point for reflection in your diary (see pages 14–15). Then expand on the thoughts and revelations that surface from them. There's no need to worry if you find it hard to come up with a possible interpretation at times: an idea may emerge at a later stage, and if not, it doesn't matter. You will still have gained a lot from the creative process in itself. And remember: no-one else knows your creations as well as you, so claim them and treasure them as your own.

EVIE'S
To her, this was a dark place, which she should leave by going straight to the light behind the white door, avoiding the red door of temptation on the right.

ROLAND'S
The white door looked like one of hope and optimism towards which he should move, in contrast to the black corridor of confusion and despair.

ANNA'S
The red door reminded Anna of her heavy past, the white door of her unknown future, and the black and blue corridor of her current indecision in life.

YOU inside

When undertaking any creative enterprise, it is important to

understand personal motivations. This section of the book gently

eases you into self-exploration, using techniques that tap into

your internal world, and that help you to confront your innermost

fears and inhibitions—of both art and of self-development.

Just relax, be honest with yourself and have fun.

1

The Scribble

The familiar scribble is a great way to ease yourself into art and bring your instinctive, creative side closer to the surface. The beauty of the scribble is that it transcends ability, so that a complete novice can create one just as easily and effectively as an experienced artist.

The simple, spontaneous scribble is something that most of us indulge in at some stage, whether we mean to or not. Developing children usually "scribble" before they can draw complete images and fully-fledged adults quite often doodle on scraps of paper. Consider how many times you have found yourself scribbling while on the phone, during a class or lecture, or at a meeting. It is likely that the scribbling action has calmed you down, released built-up tension, or just generally made you feel better.

It therefore seems a shame that these spontaneous markings are often viewed as having no creative credence. Similarly, it is a pity that, having been so absorbed in the scribbling activity, we often just discard the end result, without thinking about why we made it or what it might mean. Should this really be the case? Surely, any unconstrained marks we create on paper must speak volumes about our thoughts and emotions and should be treasured.

The scribble has been used for a long time within art therapy. Donald Winnicott, one of the leading figures in child psychology, and author of *Playing and Reality*, used the scribble effectively in his work with children by developing what he called the "squiggle game" to explore a child's psyche. Through this simple activity and interaction with his young patients, Winnicott was able to learn a

lot about them and suggest ways for them to solve their problems. His successful use of "squiggle" even led to the formation of the "Squiggle Foundation," which was registered as a charity in 1981 (www.squiggle.com). Winnicott believes that a scribble, in its capacity as an expression of primary creativity, can help you discover your sense of self. It is from this belief that the scribble projects in this book stem.

Doing the scribble activities in this chapter will afford you the opportunity to step outside the constraints of everyday verbal language and instead to express yourself in a pressure-free way through line-based images. *The Scribble within You* allows you to explore your own spontaneous scribbles; *Gestural Painting* gives you the chance to express yourself on a much larger, freer scale;

Scribble Exchange provides the opportunity for you to share your scribble experience with another person; and *Group Scribble* adds the dimension of working with several other people. Enjoy it all as you might discover more about yourself than you would have imagined possible!

Why Scribble?

Scribbling is an effective way of encouraging you into art when you are feeling unconnected, blocked and generally uninspired. It opens up creativity in many different ways.

AIMS

To expand your creativity by allowing yourself to indulge in "messy" art, thus defying convention.

MATERIALS

Sheets of white A4 paper; felt-tip pens, crayons or oil pastels.

The Scribble within You

This activity involves you taking pleasure in the creation of something initially "messy" and then transforming it into an object that you value. The process helps you to realize that every single mark you make is special, and in so doing, raises your sense of self-esteem.

1 Close your eyes and scribble freely on a piece of blank A4 paper for 3 seconds with a dark felt-tip pen, crayon or pastel. The time limit is to prevent you from developing a thought process because you should not draw as such, but just make spontaneous marks on the page.

2 Open your eyes and look at the scribble you have created until you can see something recognizable in it. You might, for example, see a face, a figure or a planet. The possibilities are endless and the choice is yours.

3 Now use different felt-tip pens, crayons or oil pastels to define and complete the image in your scribble to your satisfaction.

4 Repeat this activity three more times on separate pieces of paper, spending about 15 minutes on each image. Finish sooner if you prefer. Then spread all your images out, look at them and question yourself to see what they reveal about you. Use the questions on the right as a starting point. Keep note of any feelings or thoughts that arise in your diary.

EXPLORING *your images*

Remember when questioning yourself that there are no right or wrong answers, so any conclusions you come to are right for you:

▶ Are there any similarities in the shapes and forms you have created in each image?

▶ Are you prone to using more curves than straight lines? What do curves and circular shapes mean to you in comparison to straight lines and more angular shapes?

▶ Do you feel that the colours you used in your images reflect your mood or feelings at the time of making them?

▶ Are there themes running through your images? If so, why have these themes emerged?

▶ What aspects do you most like about your favourite images?

▶ Which images do you like least? Why is this?

AIMS

To help you open up both physically and emotionally by encouraging you to work with paint in a large-scale and free way.

MATERIALS

Very large piece of paper; masking tape or sellotape; charcoal or pencil; oil pastels, crayons, or paint and large paintbrushes; newspapers.

Gestural Painting

This activity combines the versatility of the scribble with the freedom of whole body movement. Gestural painting in the air loosens and warms up your body for your image-making on paper, resulting in more liberated artwork.

1 You may wish to do this activity outside as you will be working messily and on a large scale. However, if you are doing it inside and using paint, put down newspaper to catch any drips.

EXPLORING *your image*

This activity may seem unusual to you at first so it is good to consider its effect on you. Start by thinking about how you felt "drawing in the air" and develop your interpretation from there:

▶ Did the air painting feel silly or was it liberating? Could you have gone on indefinitely? If so, why?

▶ Did you enjoy it or did you find it awkward or embarrassing? Why do you think you felt this?

▶ Do you think the air painting helped you to create your image in a freer, less restricted way?

▶ Did you experience different emotions when drawing on paper to when air painting?

▶ Did you end up using the marks that came up in your air painting on paper or was the end result completely different?

▶ Do you view your finished painting as representative of you or your feelings? Do you like it?

2 Attach your paper to a clear wall with masking tape. If you don't have a big enough sheet, tape a number of smaller pieces together.

3 Stand in front of your paper. Close your eyes and do imaginery scribbles in the air, using large body movements. Put your whole body into the movement as if you are dancing. The scribble motions can be as little or as large as you want.

4 Then take a pencil or piece of charcoal and transfer the type of marks you have been making in the air to paper.

5 Stand away from your scribble. Study it and then use paints, oil pastels or crayons to turn it into whatever image emerges and makes sense for you. You can fill in gaps with colour, emphasize lines and add as much detail as you wish. When you have finished, think back to each step of the activity and ask yourself how it made you feel. Keep a record of these experiences in your diary.

AIMS

To see how interaction with
another person affects
your creative thinking.

MATERIALS

Sheets of white paper; pens or
pencils; colouring pencils.

Scribble Exchange

The challenge here is to turn an uninhibited scribble made by someone else into a recognizable image. So the power lies with your creative partner until you claim it as your own. Your artistic thinking may well be expanded as your partner provides you with a stimulus for thought.

1 Find a "creative" partner. Both take some paper and a pen or pencil. Shut your eyes, scribble for 3 seconds on separate pieces of paper, and open your eyes again.

2 Exchange scribbles and stare at the mark your partner has made until you can define something from it. It may be an object, a face, an animal or part of a landscape, for example. It is up to you whether you develop it into many small images or one large image.

3 Now, use colours meaningful to you to refine your partner's scribble and draw the image(s) from your mind on their paper. Repeat steps 1–3 several times to create a variety of images.

4 Lay the images before you, and observe and discuss them together. Ask each other thoughtful questions (see box, right, as a starting point) to inspire responses about the work. Then each record in your diary the outcome of the exchange.

EXPLORING *your images*

It is most important to consider your own images, rather than your partner's. Try to establish what your work touches within you. You can, however, pose searching questions to your partner to assist him or her in interpreting the images:

▶ Why do you think you chose that particular colour, shape, image or theme?

▶ Do you see any recurring patterns within your images?

▶ What associations do you have with these features?

▶ What three words would you choose to best describe each image? Why these?

▶ Which of all your images do you like best?

▶ Why do you think you like that one more than the others?

▶ Having completed the activity with your partner, what overriding feeling are you left with?

To observe how you, as an individual, relate creatively to others, in a group situation.

Very large piece of white paper; masking tape; clock or watch; felt-tip pens, crayons or oil pastels; sellotape or stapler.

Group Scribble

This activity can involve three to ten people. Together, you are led on an emotional journey: scribbling helps you to let go of inhibitions; the fantasy stage develops your powers of imagination; tearing allows a carefree action; and recreating enables you to restore a feeling of order and calm.

1 Attach the corners of your paper to an empty floor space with masking tape. Each group member should have a felt-tip pen, crayon or oil pastel, and one of you should act as timekeeper.

2 Position yourselves evenly around the paper and all scribble on it for exactly 5 minutes. Then look at the result of your scribbling.

3 Each of you imagine that you are walking into this collective scribble. Ask yourselves internal questions such as: 'Where am I? Is it safe here? Is the sun shining?' and so on. Share your experiences of this with the other group members.

4 Next, all of you tear up the image into small pieces. All stop this at the same time.

5 Each of you gather up as many pieces as you need to create your own collages on separate pieces of paper, or entirely new objects like paper necklaces or ear-rings: use tape or staples to stick the pieces of paper together.

6 Talk about the activity with the group. Record your own experience in your diary.

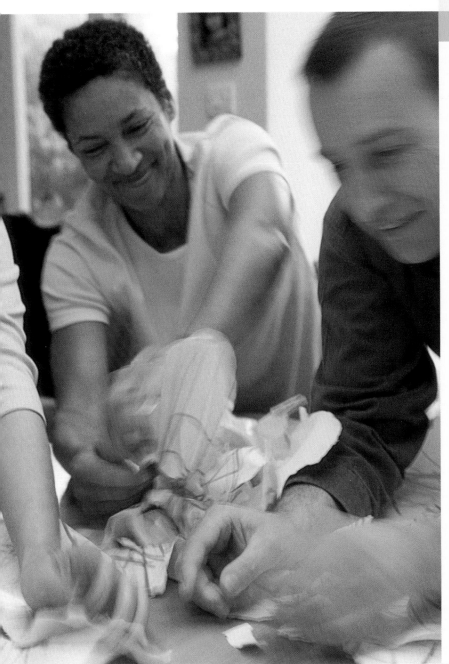

EXPLORING *the process*

This activity involves several quite varied stages, so make sure you think closely about how each of them has affected you:

▌ Did scribbling make you feel good that you were doing something unconventional with others or did you feel that you had created a mess? Does this reveal anything about you?

▌ How open or resistant were you to the idea of "walking" into the scribble? Did you feel unable to see anything in it or did other people's ideas stimulate your own imagination?

▌ How easy was it for you to tear up the paper? Did you enjoy it? Explore your energy levels when you were tearing. Did you do it carefully or was it vigorous?

▌ How did you feel creating something new at the end? Did you feel you were now reinjecting order into apparent chaos? Why did you choose to make the piece(s) you did?

Personal *insights*

PROJECT: The Scribble within You

CREATOR: Jane

Jane, a 32 year-old bookbinder, found the scribbling experience very liberating. She enjoyed putting a lot of thought into the images she was going to create from her scribbles. And she felt that her resulting fish and landscape images emerged as honest and direct.

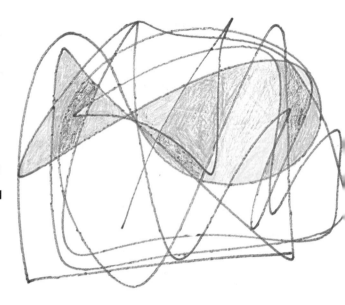

▲ *Jane found herself using mostly rounded shapes and soft yet vibrant colours in her fish image. She chose a range of blue-green shades reminiscent of the ocean.*

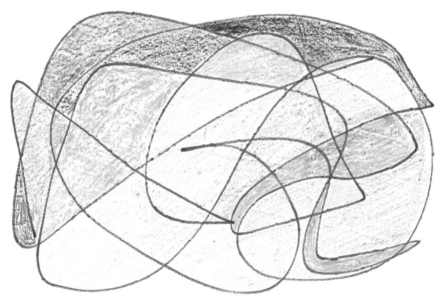

▲ *Jane's landscape image was inspired by her window-seat view on a recent plane trip. She mostly used rounded shapes and she introduced a wide spectrum of colours to fill all the space within the scribble.*

Exploring Further

Jane felt that the sea and landscape-based images expressed her appreciation of open space and lack of constraints while on a recent holiday, and the soft colours reflected her feeling of calm while there. When thinking about the rounded shapes she had used, she realized that they represented the safety and comfort she longs to feel.

PROJECT: The Scribble within You

CREATOR: Karl

Karl, a 23 year-old student, enjoyed each step of this activity, despite it raising intense emotions within him. He liked being able to take a lot of time over creating his images.

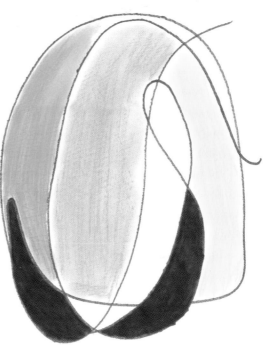

Karl came to see one of his images as a Rastafarian hat. He felt that the dark glasses hid and protected the person behind them from some exterior force.

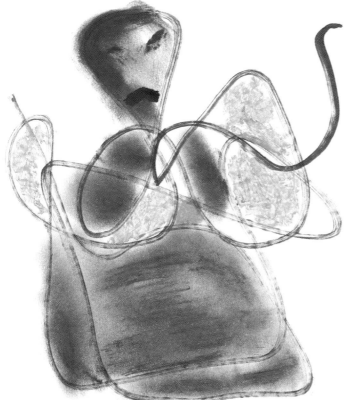

Karl's black ghost figure is scary and sinister, with a snake's head and arms that could reach out towards you. However, amidst the doom and gloom is a bright red, beating heart, which appears more positive.

Exploring Further

These images recalled to Karl a stage in his life when he felt extremely insecure. He felt the areas of black were symbolic of his feelings of helplessness, sadness and general anxiety at that time. The red heart and the bold colours in the hat, on the other hand, seemed to point to his underlying strength of character, which helped him through that difficult period.

Mind and Body

This whole book is, in a sense, about becoming more in touch with your "true self." However, this chapter, in particular, allows you to focus on new ways of using your mind and body in conjunction with art to explore your thoughts on life, and try to make some sense of them.

The mind is constantly assimilating huge quantities of information, and communicating it to the body, which then responds. However, in western society, our schooling often trains us to use the left-side of our brain or "mind" much more than the right, which means our natural instincts and creative ability become neglected and stifled, while our verbal, analytical side flourishes. With time, we start almost to fear creative processes as they seem so removed from our everyday existence—both emotionally and physically.

The activities within this chapter aim to reawaken this lost creativity and help you to regain your childhood spontaneity by stimulating and reactivating the right side of your brain.

You will be asked to think about and approach common elements of your life in a slightly different way than you usually do in order to become more in touch with your innermost feelings. For example, *Name Game* and *Dealing with Feelings* give you the opportunity to think about and represent both your name and your feelings but in terms of images instead of words; *Your Body Contour* and *Hand and Foot Painting* will lead you in the formation of artistic shapes and patterns with actual body parts rather than conventional painting tools; and *Mandala and You* and *Mandala and Problem Solving* will give you the chance to think about and recreate your

life in terms of healing circles, as this is the meaning of the Sanskrit word *mandala*. Such circles are used as religious symbols of unity and wholeness, which can help bring great balance, harmony and healing into your life. In Tibetan Buddhism, the process of making a mandala is considered as important as the end product itself—a way of calming the mind and body. Mandalas are present also in western culture, such as in the stained glass rose windows often found in Gothic cathedrals to symbolize enlightenment of the human spirit. And healing circles can be found in nature, too—flowers, spider's webs or even in tree trunks.

The famous Swiss psychologist, Carl Jung, became interested in mandalas while studying eastern religion and used them with himself and his clients as "movement towards psychological growth, expressing the ideas of a safe refuge, inner reconciliation and wholeness." The mandala-based activities within this chapter might have a similar soothing effect on you.

Why Mind and Body?

Exploring your physical and intellectual abilities and attributes is an effective step towards self-development. Mandalas are a particularly useful tool in this as they can help bring more balance into your life.

AIMS

To deepen your understanding of yourself by exploring the impact your name has had on you and your life to this point.

MATERIALS

A4 and A3 paper; pen or pencil; oil pastels or felt-tip pens; collage materials such as fabrics, scissors and PVA glue.

Name Game

This activity explores something that you probably take for granted most of the time, yet which plays quite a significant role in your life—your name. The process will help you become more in touch with your subconscious thoughts and gain a better understanding of your personal identity, past and present.

1 Take some time to think about associations with your name. Were you named after a family member or a famous person or character? Do you particularly like or dislike your name? Do people change or shorten your name, or do they call you something totally different? Have you ever felt like changing it? If so, to what would you want to change it, and how do you think others would react?

2 Write your name and any related associations on a piece of A4 paper. If you like, also use pastels or felt-tip pens to create doodles of colour, line, shape and texture inspired by your name, such as those below.

3 Now take a piece of A3 paper and create a fuller image of your name. Cut out pieces of your image, or use glue to stick on extra items, like fabric, if you want.

your name doodles can take any form you wish

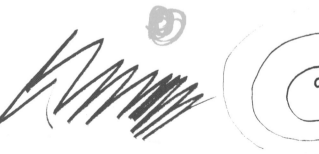

4 Look at your finished illustration and reflect on both it and the thought process behind making it. Do not be afraid to ask yourself leading questions, such as those below. Record your feelings in your diary.

EXPLORING *your image*

Doing and thinking about this activity can touch on powerful past experiences, so refer to page 11 for advice on additional support, if necessary:

❱ Which of your names did you focus on? Why this one?

❱ Was it easy to think of associations with your name?

❱ Why do you think you depicted your name in the way you did?

❱ Does your image reveal anything new about yourself?

AIMS

To identify and come to terms with any emotional and physical joy or pain you are experiencing at any given time.

MATERIALS

Piece of white paper large enough for you to lie on; a dark felt-tip pen; masking tape; paint and paintbrushes; and a friend!

Your Body Contour

Mapping out areas of joy and pain within your body allows you to engage with how you are feeling and to represent this visually. It brings to the fore any areas of concern, which can be scrutinized and worked through, and it opens the door to acknowledging the positive aspects of your life.

1 Place a large piece of paper on a clear floor space. Lie down on it in a position that reflects how you feel today.

2 Ask your friend to draw around you with a dark felt-tip pen to form an outline of your body shape.

3 Now attach your contour image to a wall with masking tape. Contemplate your image and think about areas of joy and pain that you are feeling at present. Try to maintain some kind of balance between the positive and the negative. Now decorate and colour your image appropriately. You could choose to draw or paint freely within the outline or you might prefer to work in one small section at a time. You can draw or paint in the area outside your body, too, depending on how you feel at the time. It's entirely up to you.

4 Once you've finished, stand back from your image, and reflect on what you have created and what it might mean. Record your feelings in your diary.

EXPLORING *the process*

Make sure you consider the body mapping stage of this activity as well as the drawing:

▶ How did it feel having someone draw around your body? Do you believe your body position accurately reflected your feelings at that time?

▶ What do you think about the scale of your body? Is it bigger than you had expected?

▶ Where did you begin to draw or paint and why do you think you chose to start there?

▶ Did you identify equivalent areas of joy and pain?

▶ Did you include anything that surprised you?

▶ Did you feel compelled to stay inside the contour? Why do you think this was the case?

AIMS

To allow yourself to indulge in and enjoy raw, messy creativity.

MATERIALS

Poster paint (a range of colours); large, flat paint trays; A4 and A3 white paper; large laminated board.

Hand and Foot Painting

Using hands, feet and other body parts as painting instruments can be a liberating experience. It frees you from the constraints of organized, everyday, adult life and allows you to become more in touch—literally—with your creativity.

1 Mix the paint into a thin, creamy consistency and put it in trays. Place your paper on a hard, flat surface.

2 Put the flat of your hand into the paint and make a handprint on the paper. Do this several times randomly on the page to explore as many possibilities as you can.

3 Try creating images with your handprints, such as an animal or a house. You can use any part of your hand, not only the palm of your hand and your fingers.

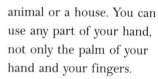

4 Then take a larger sheet of paper and do the same thing using your feet. Place the paper on the floor near the paint tray, step into the paint, and walk onto the paper. Make patterns and images just with your feet.

7 Use a dry finger to draw in the paint whatever comes to mind. Take a print of this image by placing a piece of blank paper over it and gently patting it down. Repeat this each time you create a new image.

8 Wash the paint off your hands. Display your handiwork for yourself and make decisions on what you feel did and didn't work. Remove the images that are less successful in your eyes. Explore what it is you like about the remaining images, asking yourself searching questions about your method and work (see box, right as a starting point). Record your thoughts in your diary.

5 If you're brave enough, take another sheet of paper and create images using both your hands and your feet. Always clean your hands and feet between colour changes.

6 Next, go back to using your hands only. Smear some paint onto a large laminated board with your hand to create a smooth, colourful surface on which to draw.

EXPLORING *your images*

Pose yourself questions to determine what your work reveals about your inner self:

▶ How did you feel covering your hands and feet with paint, and using them to print with?

▶ Did it feel easier with your hands or your feet?

▶ Did you find the process frustrating, as you may be used to working with tools to make your marks or images?

▶ Which piece is the most satisfactory to you? Why?

AIMS

To externalize the strong emotions
you experience, in order to maintain
a sense of balance and
self-awareness in your life.

MATERIALS

A4 and A3 paper; pencil;
colouring pencils, felt-tip pens,
oil pastels, or paint and
paintbrushes; collage materials
such as sequins and PVA glue.

Dealing with Feelings

This activity allows you to illustrate the passion you are

feeling for life at any given moment. Working on a large

surface means you can let your feelings flow at will, rather

than restricting them or keeping them bottled up inside.

You therefore give yourself an outlet for what,

at times, can be overwhelming emotions.

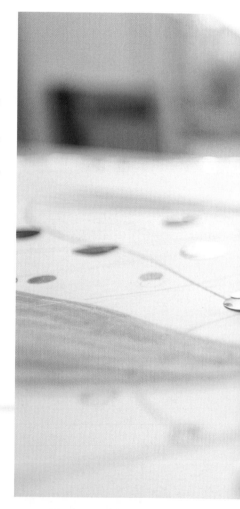

1 Think of six emotions that you commonly experience—three positive and three negative. Write each of these at the top of separate pieces of A4 paper.

2 Use a pencil to illustrate the first emotion. The best way to capture its essence is to think about the last time you felt that way. Try to relive this and then let the spontaneous feeling run through your body onto the paper. Repeat this process for each of the emotions you have written down.

3 Use line, shape, form and the intensity of your marks to confront your raw emotions and capture your true feelings. Try not to be too literal or symbolic, such as using tears for sadness or hearts for love, as these may not be appropriate for you.

4 Look at your "emotions" and decide which one you feel is most relevant to you at present. Take an A3 piece of paper and gather together materials that you feel reflect your chosen emotion.

5 Now use these materials to draw, paint or colour an image that conveys the nuances of this emotion.

6 Try not to censor your sentiments on the paper: feel free to do whatever you

YOU INSIDE

EXPLORING *your image*

Expressing raw emotion in a physical way can bring out all sorts of feelings, so make sure you consider the thought process behind your creations:

▶ Which of your initial markings were the more intense—those for positive or negative emotions?

▶ Did you find some emotions easier to depict than others? Why do you think this was the case?

▶ Why did you select the main emotion that you did?

▶ Can you see connections between the emotion and the colours and materials you used?

▶ Did you try to contain the emotion or did you let it spill all over the paper? How has this left you feeling?

▶ What do you want to do with your image—display it, keep it, throw it away, tear it up or give it away? Why is this the case?

want. If you want to cut or tear off parts of your image, do so. Alternatively, if you want to add to your image, feel free to do this, too. You could, for example, stick on pieces of fabric or coloured sequins with PVA glue.

7 Repeat the activity when you feel the need or simply at various times. Note your experiences in your diary. Make sure you talk to someone you can trust if very strong emotions are raised within this activity.

AIMS

To create a special circle that helps
you to bring equilibrium and a sense
of unity to your life.

MATERIALS

Pen or pencil; A4 paper;
A3 paper or cardboard; plate,
or piece of string and drawing
pin; scissors; oil pastels, felt-tip
pens, or paint and paintbrushes.

Mandala and You

Life can be chaotic at times, causing you
to long for balance in your life. This activity is designed
to give you the space so often needed to reflect and search
for balance and self-knowledge. Working within a mandala
that represents your universe gives you a healthy
starting point for your self-exploration.

time. If, for example, your
"fears" section has six ideas
beneath it, and your "hopes"
section only has four,
increase the latter if you
are feeling positive.

1 Think about and write down
the central aspects of your
life. Suggestions are "hopes,"
"ambitions," "fears" and
"dreams." but there are
countless other options.

2 List some specific examples
of these in your life under
each category. Try to balance
the size of your various life
categories so that they match
how you are feeling at the

3 Now draw a circle as small
or large as you wish on your
paper or cardboard base.
Either draw around a plate,
or attach a piece of string
to your pencil, and the end
of the string to the centre
of your paper with a drawing
pin. Keeping the string taut,
draw your circle with the
pencil. Once you have
finished, cut out the circle.

you can divide your mandala in any way you choose

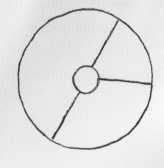
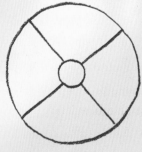

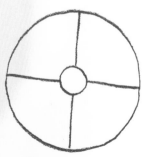

4 Using a felt-tip pen, oil pastel or paint, divide your circle into the life categories you have thought about. It is up to you how to do this. Some examples are shown bottom left but use your imagination to expand on these as much as you want.

5 Now illustrate each section to reflect how you feel about it and the elements within it. You do not have to adhere to the sections created if you don't feel like it.

6 Look at your finished work, ask yourself questions about it, and record your feelings in your diary. You might like to hang it up and use it for contemplation, as many other mandalas are used.

EXPLORING *your mandala*

Analyze how you feel about your creation by posing yourself discerning questions:

▶ Did you have more thoughts about some areas than others? Which and why? Were the same areas the easiest to illustrate?

▶ Why did you choose the categories you did?

▶ Did the process help bring some understanding into your views about yourself? Do you like your finished mandala?

AIMS

To identify problems you face
in your life and try to come up
with effective solutions.

MATERIALS

Pen or pencil; A4 paper; large
piece of white paper; oil pastels
or paint and paintbrushes

Mandala and Problem Solving

This activity allows you to think about and work through

elements of your life that you view as problematic

at any given time. Once you have identified the areas

most in need of attention, the creation of the mandala

offers you the means to search for solutions.

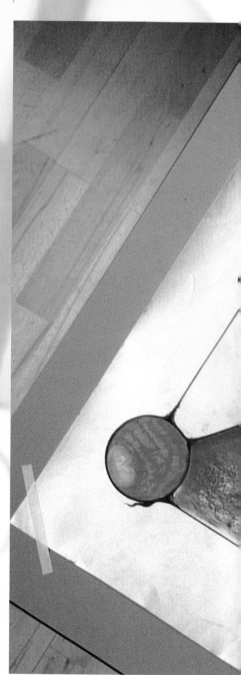

1 Take a piece of A4 paper and a pen or pencil and list the areas in life with which you feel dissatisfied at present, such as family life, friends, career or finances. Think about the factors making each of these areas worrying, and ideas for what to do to change this.

2 Take a larger piece of paper and draw a circle as big or small as you choose. You may wish to cut out your circle, or you may prefer to leave it as it is and create other shapes around it.

3 Colour and draw within your mandala to represent your problems and possible courses of action. Choose the colours and shapes that feel right to you at the time: let your instincts guide you. You either can dedicate your mandala to exploring only one problematic aspect of your life or, if there are several areas in need of attention, you can choose between creating several sections within one mandala or making separate mandalas for each issue. Record your experiences in your diary.

YOU INSIDE

EXPLORING *your mandala*

As the purpose of this activity is to try to resolve personal issues, it is crucial to ask yourself relevant questions:

▶ Was it easy to write down your problems in such a focussed way or were you reluctant to do so? Why do you think this is?

▶ Did you concentrate on one problem at a time or jump from one to another as you had ideas?

▶ Did you find it more difficult to visually represent your problems or your possible solutions? Why?

▶ Did you choose to cut out your circle? If not, did your imagery remain entirely within your circle? If yes, did working within a circle give you a sense of containing your problems?

▶ Do you feel that the creation of your mandala has helped you look at your problems in a more positive way? Has it helped you?

Personal *insights*

PROJECT: Hand and Foot Painting

CREATOR: Paul

New to art therapy, Paul found the prospect of painting with body parts quite strange. It was difficult for him at first to control the paint with his hands, but he gradually got used to this messy method. Then, when working to make a recognizable image, he started to realize through his art how important it is for him to be in control.

▼ *Paul came to enjoy the freedom of applying the paint in a spontaneous way with his hands and feet.*

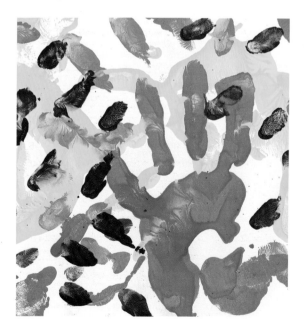

▲ *But when he tried to create something recognizable, he became anxious. He felt a need to control the image and struggled to do so. He even put a coloured border around his picture in order to contain it.*

Paul tried to make a cute animal but the red creature that emerged felt unsatisfactory. He tried again but disliked the yellow figure he made, too. Paul then introduced blue sky and green grass but still couldn't achieve the image he wanted.

When Paul got to the printing section he managed to create a bird image. He liked this and at last felt that he had gained control.

Exploring Further

Paul traced his struggle to control the images back to his childhood when both his parents had personal problems. As a consequence he was often left in a caring role, where he had to be "in control" in a difficult environment. He felt that the bird image may therefore symbolize the freedom that he missed out on at that time and that he still desires—including freedom from always having to be in control. A bird, after all, has the freedom of flight.

Personal *insights*

PROJECT: Mandala and You

CREATOR: Marcy

Marcy, whose main passion in life is art, did not imagine that the creation of her mandala would cause so much emotion to surface. Her finished product was therefore very different from what she had initially envisaged.

Marcy used repetitive sweeping motions of her paintbrush to apply many layers of paint, which gave her mandala great depth and texture. She chose several intensely rich, bright colors throughout and used them repeatedly, ending up with a mandala that had no separate sections.

On completing her mandala, Marcy was inspired to write a poem to help her cope with the pain that emerged from her past:

Fire=Pain=Pain=Fire
There is fire and there is pain,
My fire fuels my pain and my pain fuels my fire.
Without my pain there would be no fire,
Without my fire there would be no pain.
My pain fuels my fire of determination to succeed,
to achieve, to strive to move beyond my pain.
Without pain I'm not sure I would have this
amount of fire or energy.

Exploring Further

Looking back on the creation of her mandala, Marcy viewed the many layers of paint she applied as an unleashing of the layers of pain she keeps locked inside. Her use of fiery colors seemed to represent the intensity of her pain: red representing her anger and frustration, and yellow adding vibrancy and strength to it. Marcy saw a lot of fire and energy in her mandala, which influenced the choice of subject in her resulting poem. She felt that creating the mandala and the poem gave her direct access to her subconsious. By acknowledging the pain held there, she was able to start unlocking and addressing it.

PROJECT: Mandala and Problem Solving

CREATOR: James

James, a graphic designer experiencing a temporary creative block, used this activity to deal with his frustration about past negativity.

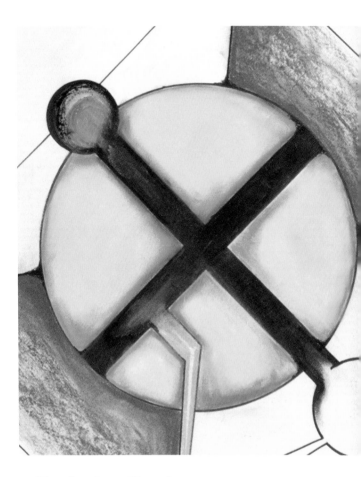

The circle of graduated blue came to represent the things that James feels he should have achieved in life, but that he has only partially managed.

He interpreted the red circle as symbolic of the strong internal rage that burns in him at times, and that he has to learn to control.

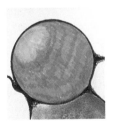

James saw the graduated orange circle as the brightness of varying degrees he feels within himself, even during the most negative times in his life.

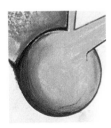

The presence of the grey turning green showed his positive outlook at the time, as green is closer than grey to the blue clarity that he desires.

Exploring Further

James realized that his mandala represented his progress through life so far: the empty circle was his negative starting point; his journey then led to a central crossroads, where the grey path that ruins the otherwise symmetrical pattern represents a bad decision he made; the corner circles (see page 54) indicate the main facets of his character (see left); and the large blue areas symbolize the clarity that he desires. The mandala helped James with his frustration at a regrettable decision by reminding him how much progress he had made since then.

Working with Clay

Clay is a tactile material that offers individuals a wide and interesting range of possibilities. The beauty of working with clay is that no intermediate tool is required to create a finished object—just you and your hands—so it offers a very immediate, and often emotive, creative experience.

The physical feeling of working with clay can evoke a wide variety of responses. Some people simply love the squidgy texture between their fingers and find the elasticity that the clay offers satisfying, and even stress-relieving. Others enjoy the process of manipulation as it means that they can create whatever form they desire and that the clay will change easily with their every wish. Other people find that they dislike the messiness and transience of working with it.

Whatever your instinctive reaction to the physicality of working with the material, it is often the case that clay's pliability creates an instant atmosphere of emotional intimacy between clay and its manipulator. The physical relationship you form with clay means that its effect on you can be instantaneous. Clay can raise all sorts of feelings and memories—whether as a result of its feel, or smell, or the objects you choose to create from it.

However, the central and most important thing during the clay projects offered in this chapter is to enjoy the experience of creating whatever you feel like, within the guidelines of each activity. Then, afterwards, try to analyze for yourself what effect it has had on you—what memories and associations it has brought to the surface, and whether you find working with clay an effective and rewarding way to express how you are feeling.

You will experience moulding clay in various ways within this chapter—using your hands to form changing shapes without thinking in *Playing with Clay*, fashioning a container you would have liked as a child in *Creating a Container*, and making a decorative plaque representing your personal qualities in *Your Personal Plaque*.

Let the fact that clay is a natural material add to the visceral experience of working with it, as this might allow you to feel close to nature while creating. You might find that you like clay's mutable aspect, as it offers you the option of flexibility where there is no need to commit to what you have made; or you might realize that its lack of immediate permanence frustrates you. Whatever your discoveries, the activities within this chapter allow you to acquire "hands-on"

experience of clay so enjoy getting stuck in! Be sure to wear old clothes when working with clay, and remember to use a suitable surface. Try not to be afraid of getting a little messy.

Why Clay?

The immediacy of clay can allow you to access deep thoughts and feelings within a very short space of time, often enabling you to go on to draw effective conclusions about yourself.

AIMS

To explore the spontaneous side
of your character by playing without
the constraint of having to make
an end product.

MATERIALS

A hand-sized ball of clay.

Playing with Clay

Often when we are developing our own creativity we forget

to enjoy the process. We become so involved in what the

end product will look like that we overlook any pleasure

or insights gained in the making. This activity lets you take

a step back and enjoy each aspect of your actions.

1 Sit comfortably on a floor cushion or chair with a ball of clay in your hands. Then close your eyes and start to play with the clay. Try not to think about making it into any specific object. Just allow yourself to enjoy handling and manipulating it.

2 Keeping your eyes closed, remain aware of the various shapes into which your hands mould the clay.

3 Open your eyes only when you feel ready. Now enjoy watching the shapes that you form. They may suggest something to you, such as a face, animal or object. If you feel a very strong urge to create this object, feel free to do so, but it is by no means the aim of the activity.

4 Reflect on the various changes experienced from the moment you started handling the clay with your eyes closed to the end of the process with your eyes open. Record in your diary any recognizable shapes you saw in your clay, along with how they, and the general playing process, made you feel.

EXPLORING *the process*

This activity gives you the opportunity to place value on a process rather than a result. It's important to question how this experience made you feel as we seldom allow ourselves the freedom simply to play as adults:

▶ Did you enjoy having the power to mold the clay into whatever forms you liked?

▶ Did you enjoy the experience of constant change and the idea that impermanence does not have to be threatening, or did you struggle with this idea?

▶ If you haven't made a specific object, does it matter to you? Why, or why not?

▶ Are you someone who believes that there should always be an end product to make an action worthwhile? If so, why do you think this is the case?

To get in touch with a particular part of your childhood and, through this, the happy, carefree child that lives within yourself.

MATERIALS

A hand-sized ball of light-coloured clay; board; poster paint and paintbrushes; old pencil; collage materials such as buttons or small toys; PVA glue.

Creating a Container

This activity helps to take you back to a happy and memorable part of your childhood, to celebrate this time, and to acknowledge positive, personal memories. Painful emotions can be stirred up, so try to steer clear of any negative elements in your childhood.

1 Put the clay on a piece of protective board and sit comfortably in front of it. Take the ball of clay in your hands, close your eyes and start manipulating it.

2 While you play with the clay, identify and dwell on a particular period in your childhood when you were happy, and of which you hold fond memories. Think about creating a container—a holder of any sort—that you would have liked at that age. What would it look like?

3 Open your eyes and mould your clay into the shape required for this container.

4 Once the shape of your container pleases you, you can decorate it if you want. An old pencil or the top end of a paintbrush are good for making marks in clay. You also can paint your container or glue on bits and pieces such as buttons if it feels appropriate. Record in your diary the emotions you experience as you create your "youthful" container.

EXPLORING *your container*

Reflecting on the past, and especially on your childhood, often raises strong emotions. It is essential to pose questions that help you deal with and learn from these feelings:

▶ How easy was it to select a happy time in your childhood?

▶ Once you had decided on an age, did the ideas flow?

▶ If you found that your memories started tumbling forth, how did it feel? Were you able to keep your thoughts on a light-hearted level? Why do you think this was the case?

▶ How did you feel while you were forming your container?

▶ Why do you think you chose to make the container you did? Do you like what you have created? Do you feel that you would have liked it even more as a child?

AIMS

To be self-indulgent by acknowledging and celebrating your uniqueness.

MATERIALS

Paper, pen or pencil; light-coloured clay, rolling pin, a tile (10 cm² or larger), knife; paint and paintbrushes; varnish.

Your Personal Plaque

We often have difficulty acknowledging the positive aspects of our own characters. The process of making this clay plaque will allow you not only to recognize your many qualities, but also to externalize them, which can lead to an increased sense of self-worth and confidence.

1 Take a few moments to think about qualities you admire in yourself. You might, for example, view yourself as very honest and reliable, or as sincere and caring.

2 Write your name in the centre of a piece of paper, and draw lots of lines branching from it. At the end of each line, write one of your attributes.

3 Contemplate your words for a minute. Then take another piece of paper and try to illustrate these qualities visually—using colour, line, shape and texture (see pages 18–25)—to capture the "essence of your being."

4 Use the rolling pin to roll out the clay to a thickness of about 5 mm. Then place your tile on it and use the knife to cut round the tile.

5 Now use implements like a pencil, a knife or the top end of a paintbrush to decorate your piece of clay with the words and/or imagery you have chosen.

6 To further express your unique qualities, you can cut and mould any surplus clay into shapes relevant to you and your feelings. Then dampen the bottoms of the shapes and lightly press them onto your clay plaque to attach them. They can be as neat or messy, and as small or large as you desire, and can be placed wherever you want on your plaque.

7 If you want to add colour to your work, leave the plaque to harden for a few days and paint it. Carefully choose your colours so they fit in with the design you have created. When the paint is dry, varnish the plaque.

8 Record any thoughts in your diary on how it felt to focus on the positive and unique parts of you.

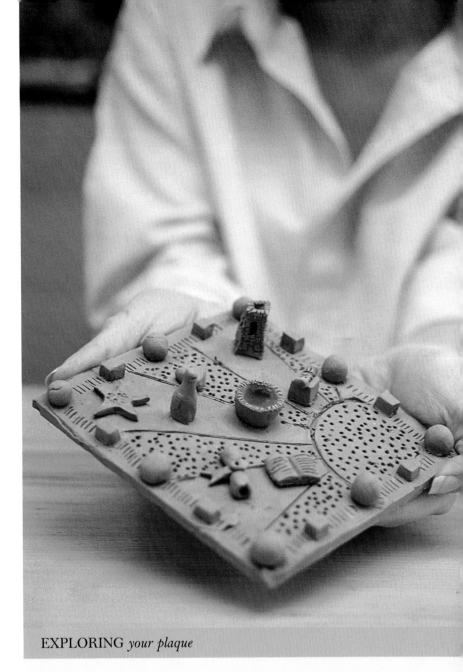

EXPLORING *your plaque*

Reflect on how it felt creating your plaque and also on what you think of the end result:

▌ Did the brain-storming session reveal unexpected sides of your character? And did it help you to create your plaque in the end?

▌ What do you think each element of your plaque says about you as a person?

▌ Are you pleased with your finished product? Or do you feel you could improve it? If so, allow yourself to do so.

Personal *insights*

PROJECT: Your Personal Plaque

CREATOR: Jane

Although Jane, an arts graduate, explored a lot about herself through making her plaque, she felt quite detached as she made it. She handled this activity on a very cerebral level, so her method of working was clean and precise.

Jane included a book as she has a constant desire to learn. Its open pages full of lines of "text" illustrate her belief that we never stop learning throughout life.

The scroll symbolizes achievement and order for Jane. Although she included it, she felt in hindsight that it was pompous and therefore regrets doing so.

She positioned a cup at the centre of the plaque, signalling her generosity of spirit and loyalty, as she feels that both these qualities are very central to her life.

Her border of neat cubes and spheres holds everything together. And although it is symmetrical, it is still fun. Again this defines her open-minded approach to life.

Sunshine radiates throughout the background of the plaque so that the rays touch all aspects of her life. This highlights how optimistic she generally feels.

Exploring Further

Each item Jane made for her plaque seemed symbolic to her. The neatness conveyed her need to stay in control, yet the sun showed her all-embracing nature. She felt the whole plaque was representative of her as it suitably depicted her love of people and positive attitude to life.

PROJECT: Creating a Container

CREATOR: Kana

Kana, who recently came to England to study, enjoyed this opportunity to explore her childhood memories of Japan. She recalled sports day in kindergarten and how she won the relay race despite having no trainers.

Having had no trainers as a child, and having longed to own a pair, Kana chose to make clay shoes as her container. She created a dainty pair of oriental-style shoes in keeping with her Japanese upbringing, and decorated them with flowers on the side and a star on the back as these images would have made her very happy as a child. She liked the fact that her end product reminded her of running when she looked at it as this was something she was good at as a child, and so gave and still gives her a sense of self-confidence.

Exploring Further

By creating a pair of shoes for the child within her, Kana fulfilled her childhood dream of owning a certain style of shoes—albeit belatedly. In presenting herself with this simple gift, she gained a real sense of self-nurturing and self-worth, which can too often be lacking in everyday adult life.

Your Dreams and Senses

Nearly all of us are blessed with the ability to touch, taste, see, hear and smell, as well as a capacity to dream. These make us feel alive and link us with our environment. Yet, while we often take them for granted, creative exploration of our dreams and senses can be a life-enriching experience.

We are continually feeding our senses, whether admiring pictures at an art gallery, enjoying a stroll in the park, eating tasty food, hugging a loved one or listening to music. Indeed, our lives are a continual cycle of striving to satisfy our senses. Yet we are often so used to them being there that we don't fully appreciate them.

Then when we are asleep, and our five normal senses are resting, another "sense" takes over—that of dreaming. The realm of dreams is an oft-visited and intriguing place for most people. Yet we tend to let these valuable, often revealing, dreams disappear into the night that brought them—due to a lack of memory or understanding.

The famous psychologist, Sigmund Freud, was one of the first scientists to explore the importance of our dreams. He saw them as windows to our subconscious minds and claimed that their every detail could shed great knowledge on our waking lives. A colleague of Freud's, Carl Jung, also believed we could learn from dreams. In fact, he discovered a lot about himself by imaging his own dreams, and therefore encouraged his patients to do the same.

Evoking a Dream gives you a chance to represent moments or themes from recent dreams in images, rather than using the usual medium of words. This lets you reproduce images directly from

your mind, giving you a more concrete starting point from which to interpret any hidden meaning in your dream. *Expanding a Dream* not only helps you to recall a dream you have had, but also to use your imagination to develop your memories by drawing possible before and after images. Bear in mind that it can be difficult to interpret dreams, but that you are always the best interpreter of your own thoughts.

The next two activities–*Orange Art* and *Touching Textures*–allow you to experience temporary sense deprivation, which will make you aware of just how much you rely on your senses. During the *Orange Art* exercise, wearing a blindfold lets you feel and taste an orange without the benefit of sight; and *Touching Textures* again removes the visual aspect–asking you to feel textures within

a sealed box or the pages of a home-made book with your eyes closed. This should provide insight into how your senses influence you on a deeper level, evoking feelings, associations and memories from the past, from which you can then produce personal artistic creations.

Why Dreams and Senses?

Exploring your dreams and senses through art not only helps you to appreciate how lucky you are in life, but also helps to open your mind, develop your powers of imagination and increase self-comprehension.

AIMS

To recall and creatively
express a dream that you
have had recently.

MATERIALS

A4 and A3 paper; oil pastels,
felt-tip pens, or paint and
paintbrushes.

Evoking a Dream

Dreams can be quite revealing, if you can manage

to remember them, that is. This activity will help you

to recapture the essence of a recent dream so that you can

try to unravel any distortion or confusion that surrounds

it and, hopefully, start to make more sense of it.

1 Take some time to recollect
as much of your dream as
possible. You may want to
write down some words,
pictures or symbols on A4
paper to jog your memory.

2 When you are ready, move
on to imagining your dream
purely in terms of colours
and shapes that represent
the events and emotions
that unfolded within it.

3 Now transfer the dream
images in your mind onto
A3 paper to create an entire
image that encapsulates
your dream. You can use
oil pastels, felt-tip pens or

paint—it is entirely up to you. Remember that it doesn't have to look ordered or make apparent sense. The whole point is to record your dream as you see it in your mind, with as much detail as you can recall.

4 Record in your diary how this dream-imaging activity has made you feel.

EXPLORING *your image*

Question yourself carefully about the process of creating a visual image of your dream, as it can be a powerful experience:

▶ How much of your dream were you able to remember? Did you get frustrated when you couldn't recall as much as you wanted?

▶ Did you choose a pleasant or unpleasant dream? What feelings did it stir up within you?

▶ Do you feel that your image truly represents your dream?

AIMS

To further develop an
understanding of
your dreams.

MATERIALS

Pen and notebook; A3 paper;
oil pastels, felt-tip pens, or paints
and paintbrushes; scissors.

Expanding a Dream

Remembering dreams is rarely easy. We think we will recall

everything on waking, but the dream fades almost

immediately. This activity will allow you to turn even

a momentary memory from a dream into something much

more detailed from which you can learn.

1 Take some time to recall
your dream. Try and
remember specific details,
and note these on paper.
It may be useful to start
keeping a pen and notebook
by your bed to jot down any
memories as soon as you
wake up each day.

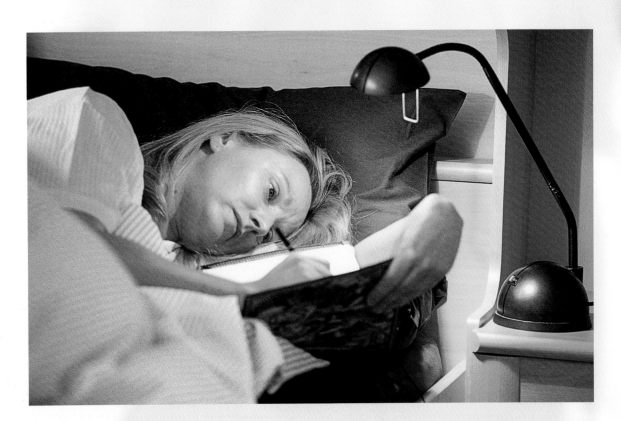

EXPLORING *your images*

This activity can be a very worthwhile one, providing great insight into your subconscious mind, so use it wisely:

▌ Why did you choose the initial dream "snapshot" that you did?

▌ Did you think much about what colours to use? Why?

▌ Once you had recalled your dream snapshot, how easy was it to think about what had or might have happened before?

▌ Was thinking of possible follow-ups to your dream easy or difficult? Did you choose one particular image or give yourself several choices?

▌ Did you increase your understanding of your dream and/or yourself by creating your series of images? If so, how?

2 Take a piece of A3 paper and draw an approximate "snapshot" of a key moment in your dream with oil pastels, felt-tip pens or paints. Be sure to use lots of imagination and colour.

3 Next think about what might have led up to this dream. Visualize the "snapshot" before the one you drew, and try to illustrate this on another piece of paper.

4 Finally create an image or images of what might have come next in your dream. There is no right or wrong to this—do whatever feels authentic. You can cut out your images if you want.

5 Once you have all your images before you, choose the dream image you like best. Reflect on why this might be. Record your feelings in your diary.

AIMS

To heighten your senses and develop your creativity with the use of one colour alone.

MATERIALS

An orange; blindfold; knife; A3 card or paper; paint and shallow paint tray; PVA glue.

Orange Art

An orange lends itself to the stimulation of four of our five senses: its peel has a distinctive texture for our hands to touch, its bright colour gives our eyes a visual treat, there's a very tangy aroma, and it has a sweet taste when eaten. Enjoy the opportunity this activity gives to explore these elements.

1 Wash your hands and the orange before you start. Put on a blindfold, and enjoy feeling, squeezing and smelling the orange. Lick and bite it, too, if you want to experience the peel. Remove the blindfold and note in your diary how these actions felt. Then relive the actions without the blindfold. Do they feel different now?

2 Next, cut your orange in two. Touch, smell and taste it again, and note how this experience compares to the same actions when the orange peel was on.

3 Cut one orange-half in half again. Pour paint into the paint tray, dip an orange section into the paint, and use the orange to print on some card or paper. Do this with all the various sides and sections of the orange to use it effectively as a painting tool. Continue on separate pieces of paper, if you want.

EXPLORING *your images*

Ask yourself appropriate leading questions about this exploration of your senses:

▌ How do you feel about the colour orange in general?

▌ Do oranges remind you of certain places or events?

▌ Which part of this activity did you enjoy most?

▌ How did you find printing with such an unconventional tool?

▌ Do you like your final images?

4 Once you have finished creating your image(s), you can peel your orange and glue pieces of the rind to your paintings, or use them to make a collage on another piece of paper.

5 Study your final images to see how you feel about them and the method of image-making you have just used. Use your diary to note all your findings.

AIMS

To explore the feel and texture
of a variety of materials with
a view to reminiscing.

MATERIALS

Sheets of card or a cardboard
box with lid; materials such as
fabric and foil; holepunch; ribbon
or string; scissors; PVA glue;
tape; paint and paintbrushes.

Touching Textures

This activity focuses on your sense of touch. Closing your

eyes and feeling varied textures with your hands alone can

transport you back in time, and allow you to recall

or relive memories and hidden emotions.

1 Gather together about ten
differently textured
materials. Then decide
whether you want to make a
"feely box" into which you
dip your hand or a "feely
book" that you flip through.

2 If you want to make a box,
cut a hole in one side of
your cardboard box that is
big enough to get your hand
through, but not big enough
to let you see the contents.
If you can see through the
hole, attach some loose
material to cover it that still
allows you to put your hand
inside (see left).

3 If you choose to make a
book, punch holes at the
edge of ten sheets of card.
Then thread through ribbon
or string, and tie the ends.

4 Next, cut out your textured
materials. You do not have to
use fabrics, you can also
choose things like straw and
pipe cleaners if you want.

5 Then open your box or your home-made book and assemble your textured materials in any fashion you want, making sure that you glue them down inside so that they do not come loose when touched later.

6 You can paint and/or decorate the outside of your box or book to satisfy your sense of sight, too.

7 Once you have finished, close your eyes. Then put your hand through the hole in the side of your box or flick through your book to feel all the textures. Make a note in your diary of how each of them makes you feel. A texture may trigger, for example, thoughts about a person, a place or a previous time in your life.

8 You might even be inspired by your textures to produce a piece of creative writing or a drawing to explore your feelings further.

EXPLORING *your textures*

Don't worry if no texture associations emerge immediately. Take time to question yourself:

▶ Did you decorate the outside of your box or book? Why?

▶ How did it feel being led by your sense of touch alone?

▶ What sensations did each texture you felt give you?

▶ Would you want to share your box or book with others to see how it affects them?

Personal *insights*

PROJECT: Expanding a Dream

CREATOR: Samantha

A multimedia lecturer, Samantha was delighted at how much she was able to develop and learn from the momentary snapshot she had remembered of her recent dream.

▲ Samantha knew that the great, golden lion would not give up in its quest to get in, and that she would not be strong enough to keep it out.

▲ In her dream snapshot Samantha saw herself as a vulnerable ten-year-old child, desperately trying to hold her bedroom door shut as an enormous lion tried to push through and get in. Her wide-eyed expression and open, screaming mouth show her true terror and panic.

The image Samantha created for the scene before this moment was of herself at her bedroom window, terrified at the thought of the lion approaching the house from her garden. She then imagined herself running to the door to try to close it and stop the lion from getting in.

Samantha thought of two possible endings. In the first, the lion got into the room but was much smaller than she had imagined, which meant she easily squashed it with her foot.

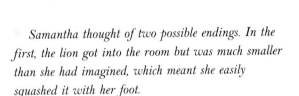

In the second imaginary ending to her dream, the lion got in again but, this time, she managed to calm it down and even end up gently stroking it to sleep.

Exploring Further

Samantha felt that her dream was stress-related. She saw the lion as representative of undefined things or people that she fights to keep out of her life due to fear of confrontation. She preferred her second ending to her dream, in which she made friends with the lion, who turned out to be much less frightening than she had imagined. Samantha learned that confronting her fears may be the best way forward for her, because her fears are seldom as terrifying as she builds them up to be. She was excited at the prospect of trying to put this realization into action.

Personal *insights*

PROJECT: Touching Textures

CREATOR: Kate

Kate, a 32-year old, decided to make a "feely box" as she loved the idea of her chosen textures being contained within something solid, and therefore not being visible even if she was to open her eyes. This meant that her sense of touch alone would be stimulated and heightened by the materials.

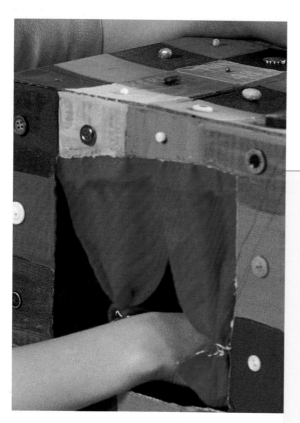

On viewing her finished feely box from the outside, Kate felt that it looked like a stage with curtains. The bright colours and golden buttons made her think of fun theatrical productions like circus shows.

Kate had used a real assortment of different textures inside the box: rushes, feathers, velvet, spaghetti and even a bath-sponge. On placing her hand inside the box, the rushes reminded her of walking in the woods with her family, an experience that she always found comforting; the feathers made her feel happy, comfortable and free, a state of mind encompassing positive relationships; and the velvet brought back her childhood need for constant affection. In contrast, the spaghetti revived unhappy memories of the confusion she felt at school, and a bath-sponge, for some reason unknown to her, made her feel extremely uncomfortable, evoking mistrust and lies.

Exploring Further

Kate's theatrical "feely box" contained much diversity. The soft patches and hard surfaces within the box left her with a reminder that there are both positive and negative elements to everything in life. She was pleased that she painted her box as she did, as it depicted her life as fun, colourful and inviting to others. Kate was surprised, however, that so many mixed memories emerged from this project, together with deep feelings about relationships and life, and wanted to consider these issues in more detail at a later stage.

PROJECT: Touching Textures

CREATOR: Anna

Anna, a social worker, decided to create a "feely book" as she wanted to be able to carry her creation around with her and experience its varied materials whenever she felt like it. She enjoyed choosing and feeling the textures within it as most of them evoked memories of her childhood in Ireland.

The purple, jagged-edged square of velvet was reminiscent of a soft carpet from a house in which she had lived with her mother and grandmother as a child.

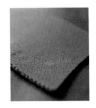

The collection of beans evoked a memory of her sister, aged two, with a broken arm caused by her falling against a pebble-dashed wall while the two played outdoors.

The bubblewrap reminded her of the innocence of childhood play— she and her sister playing happily on the cold tiles of the kitchen floor, with not a care in the world.

The piece of bright net brought to the fore memories of her father, who was a fisherman by trade. She remembered looking forward to him coming home each night as it meant he had returned safely from sea.

Exploring Further

For Anna, this activity really was a trip down memory lane, particularly into her early childhood. She was surprised that so many distant events were brought to life simply by feeling the textures that she had chosen. The experience delighted her as it allowed her to appreciate once again what a happy, carefree childhood her family had given her. She felt that she would like to go on to consolidate the experience later by using her thoughts and diary notes as the basis of a poem.

YOU outside

Mask-making

Assemblages

Ceremonies and Rituals

Living in society with other people inevitably adds richness to
our lives, as well as creating some tensions. This section
explores how each of us relates to and interacts with others on
a daily basis. The activities here focus on the enormous impact
that external events, objects and people have on our lives,
as well as on how we present ourselves to others.

Mask-making

The use of masks is widespread in many cultures. In addition to symbolic tribal masks, and flamboyant festival ones, we all assume invisible masks in our everyday lives. This chapter lets us take a closer look at the multiple roles masks play in our lives, and how we can use them to our full advantage.

In ancient times the power of the mask was much respected. In fact, mask-wearers were often thought to be imbued with special powers. Wearers of the Sri Lankan devil masks, for example, were said to stave off disease; and Native Americans used the power of masks to bring about changes in weather and victory in battle.

On a more practical level, masks have always offered protection, such as the armour of knights, and the face coverings of sportsmen. Masks are also a traditional form of disguise, whether for highwaymen, modern burglars, or people at masquerade balls. And for women, masks tend to be associated with modesty, as demonstrated by the wearing of the bridal veil or the chador. Masks also have been traditionally employed in theatrical productions, notably in ancient Greek plays and the Noh theater of Japan, where they represent specific characteristics.

We also adopt invisible masks in our daily lives—both consciously and subconsciously—to conceal certain parts of ourselves and project others, depending on situations. The "masks" we present at work, to our friends and to our family are all very different, and each of these reveals a different side of our character. Seldom do we remove them all, but, when we do, it can be both liberating and frightening, as it is only then that our true self is revealed.

Masks also play an important role in festivals. Carnival, as perfected in Brazil and the Caribbean, is a fantastic forum for people to let themselves go and take on bolder personas. Carnival preparation is highly creative, defies conventional ways of seeing, and gives people scope to be as exotic, flamboyant and outrageous as possible. When the masks go on, all inhibitions are off.

This chapter gives you a chance to create your own face and body masks, in order to bring out sides of yourself that you usually keep private, to present yourself in any light you want, and, ultimately, to increase your self-confidence. *Half-face Mask* allows you to think about your personality traits and broaden your self-perception; *Full-face Mask* lets you develop another side to your character or adopt an entirely different persona; *Whole Body Mask* encourages you to consider how you feel about your appearance; and *Carnival Costume* draws you into a party spirit and encourages you to choose and transform yourself into a fantasy character.

Why Masks?

Mask-making and wearing is a remarkably powerful way of unlocking your inhibitions and allowing the varying, sometimes unexpected, sides of yourself to emerge. It can be a truly liberating experience.

AIMS

To explore different sides of your
personality and challenge your
perceptions of yourself.

MATERIALS

Ruler or measuring tape; paper
and pen; pieces of card;
scissors; oil pastels, or paint
and paintbrushes; PVA glue;
holepunch; elastic.

Half-face Mask

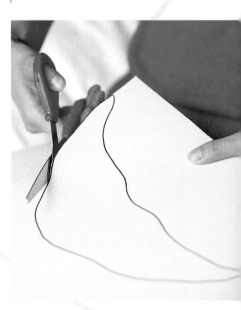

Traditionally worn as disguises, masks allow you to lose a lot

of inhibitions and self-imposed expectations. You might

choose to make a mask that hides certain negative aspects

of your character or one that highlights your positive traits.

Whether you choose to create one for the top half or the

bottom half of your face may, in itself, say a lot about you.

1 Decide whether you want to make a mask for the top or bottom half of your face, or indeed one for each half.

2 Measure the width of your face at the appropriate place with your fingers, a measuring tape or a ruler. Then, on a piece of paper, draw a template of the appropriate size. Design your own shape of half-mask, as simple or elaborate as you want. Cut out the template so that you can use the same shape to make other masks at a later date if you want.

3 Place your template on a piece of card, draw around it and cut it out.

4 Hold your mask to your face to find where your eyes or lips are, depending on which half of your face it is covering. Draw them in place and cut them out.

5 Then decorate your mask by adding colour and pattern to it with paints or oil pastels. Glue on extra elements if you desire, such as sequins, beads or any other available odds and ends.

6 Finally, you need a way to wear your mask. To attach it to your face, punch a hole at each side, thread a piece of ribbon or elastic through the holes, cut it to the relevant length, and knot the ends to keep it firmly in place.

7 Put on your finished mask in front of a mirror. If you have made two masks, try them on separately, as well as together. Spend more time in the one you find most difficult to wear.

8 Have fun in your mask(s) to see how you feel. Try talking to yourself in the mirror, read aloud a poem, make up a fantasy story inspired by your mask(s), or do a dance with it (them) on. Make sure you keep a record of the experiences and their impact on you in your diary.

EXPLORING *your half mask*

Stepping outside of your normal self can be a very rewarding experience so try to gain as much from it as you can:

▶ If you made only one mask, why do you think you chose to cover that half of your face?

▶ Did covering only part of your face feel odd? If so, why do you think this was the case?

▶ Did your mask end up flamboyant and exotic or quite understated? Think about why.

▶ How did you feel when role-playing in your mask?

▶ Did this activity allow you to explore a side of your character that doesn't normally come to surface? Were you surprised at how your mask made you feel?

AIMS

To temporarily transform yourself
into a new persona in order to
improve your self-confidence.

MATERIALS

Ruler; paper; pen; scissors; card
or cardboard box; oil pastels or
paint and paintbrushes; collage
materials such as wool and
rubber bands; PVA glue.

Full-face Mask

Wearing a mask can be a very powerful experience that gives you the opportunity to become whatever you want for a while. The fact that your whole face will be hidden behind the mask you create in this activity will give you the freedom to speak and act out of character which, in turn, can develop your personality and raise your self-esteem.

1 Spend a few moments thinking about a character that you would like to become, whether a person, animal or fantasy creation. Alternatively, pick a positive personality trait that you would like to develop.

2 Select and gather together materials to make a mask that will represent this. You might choose to make a flat mask out of card, or you may prefer to make a box mask that covers your entire head. It is entirely up to you, so use your imagination.

3 Measure the length and width of your face with a ruler. If making a flat mask, draw a shape on card that pleases you and cut it out. If making a box mask, be sure that the box you choose fits comfortably over your head.

4 Put on your mask and mark your eyes, nose and lips by feeling where they are. Cut them out if you want.

5 Decorate your mask by introducing colour to it with oil pastels or paints. Be as bold as you like. If you use paint, let it dry.

6 You can then add features like ears, a nose, a snout or hair, using wool, rubber bands or paper. A simple tip for making curly hair out of paper is to cut thin strips and wind them around a pencil before attaching.

7 Try on your mask. Have a conversation with your new persona in the mirror, or interview it to find out more about it. This will allow you to explore parts of yourself through your mask. Record the whole interaction with the mask in your diary.

EXPLORING *your mask*

It is important to consider the effect that this revealing activity has had on you:

▶ What type of mask did you choose to make? Look at your choices and trace why you think you have made them.

▶ Look at the characteristics of your mask. What features did you emphasize most? Why do you think you did this?

▶ How did it feel talking to your new persona in the mirror?

MATERIALS

Large pieces of card; pen;
scissors; oil pastels or paint and
paintbrushes; collage materials
such as felt; PVA glue;
holepunch; string.

Whole Body Mask

A mask is often associated with the face alone. However, it

can cover part or all of your body as well, and may be in one

part or in lots of sections, like any costume. Before you start

making it, think about its intended purpose—is it to hide,

decorate or draw attention to you? Make sure you focus on

positive elements of yourself, rather than just negative ones.

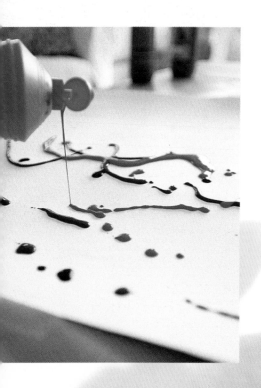

1 There are several ways of
approaching this type of
mask. Begin by gathering all
the materials for your mask
around you. You could
create shapes in whatever
order feels right at the time
as you stand amidst your
materials. Alternatively, you
could lie down on a large
piece of card, get someone
to draw around you, and cut
out this shape to use as a
base. Or you could think
about how you feel about
various parts of your body
and create pieces to match
the thoughts that emerge.

2 Once you have created the
base shape(s) of your choice
using one of these methods,
start to decorate it/them as
creatively as you like. Use
oil pastels or paint to add
colours and patterns that
reflect your body mask's
purpose and theme.

3 Glue on extra features, such
as felt and glitter, to give
your mask more depth,
texture and character if
it feels right to you.

4 If you have a number of sections to your body mask, decide whether you want to attach them all together. If so, use a holepunch to pierce holes in the ends of the card and attach them together with string. Also decide whether you want to attach the mask to your body and how to do this.

5 Having completed your mask, put it on. Consider how it makes you feel. It doesn't matter what others may think if they were to see you in it. It's what you think and feel that's important. Enjoy wearing it.

6 Then look at yourself in the mirror. Try dancing and singing in your mask, too. Note down in your diary your feelings and thoughts throughout the activity.

EXPLORING *your body mask*

Having made and worn your body mask, consider what you have learned about yourself from the experience:

❯ Which method did you use to make your body mask? Why did this method appeal to you?

❯ How much of your body did you wish to cover? What were the reasons for your choices?

❯ How elaborate were you when decorating? What are the dominant colours that you used?

❯ Why did you choose the collage materials you did?

❯ How did it feel to put on your mask? Would you be happy to show yourself to someone else and interact with him or her in your mask? Could you perform with your mask on?

❯ Did you feel like yourself in your mask or like a different person? What feelings were you left with after the activity?

To throw caution to the wind, shrug off all inhibitions, and allow yourself to live out a fantasy.

Large pieces of card or material; scissors; felt-tip pens, oil pastels, or paint and paintbrushes; collage materials such as feathers and beads; PVA glue.

Carnival Costume

A carnival costume allows you to shed your restrictive clothing and ideas, and instead adopt a persona that encapsulates the care-free spirit of the event. By transforming yourself into something that you may have longed secretly to become for years, you can open your mind and reveal an entirely new side to yourself.

1 You may wish to share this mask-making session with friends and play suitable music. It's a good idea to wear old clothes so that you can attach accessories onto them without worry.

2 Each person should think of a creature or spirit he or she would like to become, and gather appropriate materials. Think large, free, light, colourful and extravagant.

3 Cut out base shapes that will fit your bodies, whether in card or cloth. You can colour these with paints, oil pastels or felt-tip pens if you want. Then attach other objects, such as feathers, leaves and tissue paper. Use your creativity to make each of your costume items unique.

4 Once the costumes have been created, put them all on and make an occasion of it with some food, drink and dancing. Note in your diary how it has felt to become your carnival character, and discuss it with your friends.

EXPLORING *your costume*

The fantasy lived out within this activity can result in all sorts of realizations about yourself and how you interact with others, so make sure you question yourself about the whole experience:

▶ How long did it take you to think of a theme for your carnival costume?

▶ Did your ideas flow freely while making the costume?

▶ Do you feel the presence of others liberated or inhibited you? Why do you think this was?

▶ Did your feelings to the costume change once you started partying?

▶ Do you think that you interacted differently with your friends as a result of wearing your costume? How did others respond to it?

▶ Has this experience helped build your confidence?

Personal *insights*

PROJECT: Carnival Costume

CREATOR: Chloe

Chloe, a television producer, had a great time making her costume. She used it as a chance to transform what she views as her very plain outward appearance into her dream of a more vibrant facade, which more accurately reflects her inner spirit and passion for life.

▷ *Chloe decided to transform herself into a bird-like creature as she would love to fly around the universe. She combined fire and lightning motifs associated with the story of the rebirth of the phoenix, with calming blues and greens of the ocean. These elements, combined with thinking about the changes taking place in her media career at the time and the energy created during a carnival, inspired her to make her bright, exotic, flamboyant and feathery bird mask and wings.*

Exploring Further

Chloe found the whole creative process both fulfilling and empowering, especially as it was shared and then experienced with others in the fun spirit of carnival. She loved the balance she achieved between inspiration from her own imagination and from nature, through the thematic presence of fire, water and animals. She took particular pride in the sense of energy and movement she managed to capture with her choice of colours, patterns, shapes and materials as wearing her costume gave her the feeling of freedom and passion that she strives for and dreams of in everyday life.

PROJECT: Whole Body Mask

CREATOR: Sara

Sara built several "body masks" based on how she felt about different parts of her body. She loved the idea of creating and hiding behind a whole outfit as she had never felt very confident about her face and body. This project allowed her to revel in making choices for aesthetic reasons only, which she usually tries to prevent herself from doing elsewhere in life.

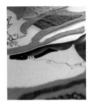

Sara decorated her body mask very elaborately, and enjoyed working with abstract shapes and cutting out different patterns. The pinks, lavender and purple she used seemed romantic, rich and feminine to her. And she thought that the soft texture of the felt used depicted her sensitivity and love for the tactile aspect of things.

Sara, who is in her early 20's, initially felt silly in her face, tunic and skirt mask, but her confidence grew with the anonymity they gave her. She felt that she could happily interact with another person while wearing it, but would have preferred it if that person wore a mask too, as both people would be shrouded in mystery. She also felt that she could perform in it, but again, more comfortably if her true identity were to remain hidden throughout.

Exploring Further

Looking back at her creation, Sara was delighted with it. She saw her body mask as sensual and mysterious, as well as very representative of certain aspects of her middle-eastern culture. The face mask reminded her of the veil that middle-eastern women often have to wear, which can be so alluring, despite its intended purpose of concealment. This is because it reveals the eyes only— arguably the most expressive feature of the body. Sara was particularly pleased that the mask looked so bright and optimistic as she felt this accurately conveyed her love of life and art.

Assemblages

Modern life has provided us with hundreds of objects that have a potential place in artistic creations but that get thrown away after little use. This chapter is designed to allow you to explore your own associations with the everyday objects you encounter, as well as make recycling personally rewarding.

Items such as fabric remnants, plastic cups, cardboard boxes and found objects are great to use in the creation of assemblages. Collecting and re-using everyday items not only saves you from having to spend time and money buying specialist materials, but also helps you to avoid the guilt so often experienced when throwing away things you've hardly used. And there is an added bonus of enjoying the experience and, indeed, the challenge of creating something out of nothing.

The use of commonplace objects in collages and three-dimensional objects gained particular status in the Surrealist, Cubist and Pop Art movements. As far back as 1912, Picasso made constructions from disparate objects such as cardboard boxes, paper and pieces of wood. Artists such as Andy Warhol and Robert Rauschenberg also dabbled in creating art from found and ordinary materials. Warhol, for example, painted and printed a Campbell's soup can as his subject. He used this as it reminded him of the feelings of warmth and comfort his mother had always given him by serving Campbell's soup for lunch every day. And later in his career, he started to incorporate his wigs into works of art by framing them. Rauschenberg, in the 1950s, used torn newspaper, pieces of cloth and objects such as umbrellas to define the struggle between life and art in his collage paintings. He caused quite a stir with *Bed* in

1955, a painting reinforced with actual bed clothes, such as a quilt and pillow, and painted over to suggest passion. Present-day artists like Tracy Emin, who also created a bed installation, use similar techniques to great effect.

The activities within this chapter enable you to explore you own associations with, and view of, the objects that surround you on a daily basis. *Magazine Collage* encourages you to take apart and re-create already-printed images in order to make something entirely new and personal from them; *Kitchen Collage* gives you a chance to see how you feel about experimenting with dried foodstuffs in your art; and *Your Personal Box* asks you to make a box that represents how you view yourself and how you think others view you—purely from everyday objects you find in the house.

Assemblages are a very accessible form of art as you need no specialist materials or actual artistic skills. You can just have fun collecting objects, choosing from your collection and putting them together to create something new and exciting.

Why Assemblages?

Making use of materials other than paint and paper can open up a whole new dimension to your creativity, as well as inspiring you to look at everything around you as an object of potential beauty and value.

AIMS

To become aware of how you can
contribute creatively to recycling.

MATERIALS

Old magazines; scissors; white
paper or card; oil pastels or
felt-tip pens; PVA glue.

Magazine Collage

Making a collage is simple and yet can be very absorbing, creative and, ultimately, satisfying. You select striking images and words from publications, remove these from their contexts, and reposition them to form an entirely new image.

1 Look through some old magazines and cut or tear out words and images that immediately catch your eye. Do not think too much at this stage about what you might do with them.

2 Next get a sheet of paper or card and lay out beside it all the images you have chosen.

3 Select the images that you want to use and decide whether to cut them further or use them in their entirety. Place and glue them wherever you like on the paper: you could cover the entire page; you could draw a shape with an oil pastel or a felt-tip pen and glue your images within this; or you could cover the whole surface, draw a shape on the back of it, and cut this out. You might then want to mount your cut-out collage on another piece of paper.

4 Once you have completed this activity, record your feelings in your diary, using the questions on the right as a catalyst for your thoughts.

EXPLORING *your magazine collage*

Considering each stage of this activity will help you understand your subconscious better:

▌ Did you choose to cut or tear out your images? Did you always cut out the things you found most compelling? What can you deduct from this?

▌ Why did you choose the images and words you did? Can you make links between them?

▌ Did you create a recognizable shape with your cut-out pictures? What do you think of your finished collage? What do you want to do with it now?

▌ Did you find this activity satisfying? Has the process made you more aware of how much waste there is in modern, consumer society?

AIMS

To expand your creativity and
concept of art by working
with foodstuffs.

MATERIALS

Differently shaped, dried pasta;
dried peas and beans; rice,
coffee beans, etc.; thick card;
pencil; PVA glue and old spatula.

Kitchen Collage

Art can be created using all sorts of materials: there is

no need to be conventional. Pasta comes in various exciting

shapes but, on the whole, is not colourful; while lentils are

bright and colourful but identically shaped—so by combining

these and other kitchen staples you can form all sorts

of beautiful patterns and images.

1 Spread out your pasta, beans
and other materials to see
the array of colours and
shapes before you.

2 Lay your piece of card in
front of you. Spread ample
glue on the card with a
spatula and start placing
your objects on top. If,
however, you would like to
create a landscape or some
other recognizable image, it
is best to do a light sketch
with a pencil on your card
before you apply the glue
section by section.

3 Then start placing objects
on the card. You can add
them one at a time to form
patterns or, if you intend to
cover a larger area, you
could sprinkle the pieces on
more randomly. It depends
how neat and organized you
want your design to be.

4 If you are creating a specific
picture, like a landscape, try
to use colour and texture to
suggest various parts of the
image, such as green peas
for hills, rice for clouds and
orange lentils for crops.

5 When you have finished,
leave your image to dry for
a while. Then spend a few
minutes looking at your
image and note what you
feel about it. Write your
observations in your diary.

EXPLORING *your kitchen collage*

Using foodstuffs as the basis of artwork can seem strange at first so it is important to think about how exactly it made you feel:

▶ Did you enjoy using food to create your image? Or did you find it limiting and wasteful?

▶ How do you feel about the textures in your image? Did you enjoy the feeling while doing it?

▶ Did you think you used the colour and shape of the materials in the best way you could?

▶ Have you created a random pattern or something recognizable? Is there any reason why you chose to do so?

▶ Are you pleased with your finished collage? Why do you think this is the case?

AIMS

To think about how you project
yourself to the outside world.

MATERIALS

A box; paper; felt-tip pens, or
paint and paintbrushes; scissors;
glue; tape; string; collage
materials such as coloured paper,
fabric, tissue paper and ribbon.

Your Personal Box

Creating a box representative of yourself allows you to

explore how you view yourself and how you feel others see

you. Including both internal and external characteristics will

give you insight into how much you keep locked away from

people and why, leading to increased self-understanding.

1 Select a cardboard box that
appeals to you. Make a
conscious decision about its
volume, shape and size,
rather than simply picking
any old box that you have
nearby. Alternatively, you
could make your own box
from cardboard or other
suitable material.

2 Take a few moments to think
about the main aspects of
how you feel you present
yourself to others. Write
them down on A4 paper.
Then do the same for the
aspects of yourself that you
feel you keep hidden away.

3 Gather together materials
that you feel reflect these
ideas and with which you
would like to decorate your
box. Then set to work
decorating it. You can start
on the inside or outside,
depending on how you feel.
You might want to paint or
colour your box before you
do anything else or you may

prefer to cut bits out of it, or glue things onto it as it is. Your box could have lots of separate sections if you want, and you might make these sections easily accessible or very difficult to get to, depending on what feels right at the time. Feel free to put whatever you desire inside the box.

4 It is easy to get carried away with this activity, so try and give yourself a time limit, or give yourself breaks between the stages of creation. You might even want this to be an ongoing project that you work at over time. Note down any refelections in your diary throughout the creation process, and record any emotions that surfaced.

EXPLORING *your personal box*

You can use this fulfilling activity to learn a lot about yourself:

▌ Think about why you chose the box you did. How does it relate to you and your life?

▌ Does the outside capture how you feel you are seen by others, or is it how you see yourself?

▌ Is the inside very different from the outside? Why do you think it has turned out like this?

▌ Did you spend more time on the outside or inside of your box? Why was this the case?

▌ Have you gained any new insights into your feelings?

Personal *insights*

PROJECT: Your Personal Box

CREATOR: Susan

A book editor, Susan enjoyed devoting a lot of time to making her box. She saw it as a chance to spend precious time on herself and give herself a "gift" to celebrate her life. Creating it not only allowed her creativity to flow but also taught her a lot about herself.

Susan made a solid, neat, little white box that illustrated beautifully how other people tend to see her— a white, middle-class pillar of society who is reliable, stoical and very reserved. She then chose to create little sections—boxes within the box—that sit on top of one another and can be pulled out carefully using a ribbon that she attached. She decided to dedicate three boxes to herself (below), one to her mother (opposite, top) and one to her father (opposite, bottom).

She filled her mother's box with a mini American flag to represent her American upbringing, a beautiful black and white photo of her as a younger woman, blank, white price tags to represent their days out shopping together, and a piece of pretty, flowery fabric to acknowledge all the positive things her mother has given her through life. All this was topped off by a sky-blue lid decorated with flecks of gold and silver, which completed an intriguing and inviting little box.

Her father's box turned out quite differently. It contained a photograph of him, as well as a mini soccer ball and a lump of dried bread. Susan felt that these items accurately depict her father's main interests in life. She finished the box by giving it a lid of gold and black checks that looked somewhat like a chess board, implying reserve, precision and finality.

One of Susan's own boxes (far left) shows her dislike for violence, hypocrisy and greed. She wishes that people could love each other, rather than treat each other badly. This is well illustrated by the fact that her box has angry, red and grey scribbles as well as holes and slashes on the lid, in contrast to the delicate flowers, star-shapes and bright ladybird within it.

Susan filled her plain white box (middle left) with a mass of coloured threads, which she feels reveals her general feeling of lack of identity and direction in life.

She made her gold-lidded box (left) to celebrate living in a free, democratic society. The flags, the multi-coloured plasticine ice cream, the silver hearts and the pieces of gold paper are symbolic of the opportunities surrounding her, which she so values having in her life.

Exploring Further

Susan was truly delighted with the box of treasures that she had made for and about herself. She found the huge contrast between the inside and outside of her box of most interest. It made her realize the extent to which it frustrates her that people are so quick to judge on outer appearance only, without taking the time to look deeper for the life and passion that lies inside everyone and everything.

Ceremonies and Rituals

Significant occasions like weddings and funerals, and even everyday routines like cooking certain meals, are usually marked by ritualistic or ceremonial behaviour. The creative activities in this chapter can make you question accepted traditions, and offer you a new approach to life.

In almost all societies, past and present, beginnings, endings and key moments are marked and honoured by rituals. Ceremonies are often our way of trying to impose external order on our lives, in the hope that it will give us a sense of peace and inner balance. So if we don't have the opportunity to express our feelings at such times, we might experience a sense of fragmentation in life.

Ritualistic behaviour is present in our everyday lives, from how we greet people, to set patterns at work, and even to a favoured night-time tipple. Religion has played a major part in the evolution of many other rituals, from candle and incense burning, to circumcision in the Jewish and Muslim religions. However, even traditional ceremonies, like weddings, can vary greatly according to each country, culture or religion.

The use of medicine wheels is another example of a traditional ritual. For the Native Americans, the medicine wheel was a sacred symbol, used to indicate the continuous cycle of the universe: change, life, death, birth, and learning. It was believed to help people explore their internal worlds, and gain inner peace, spiritual strength, and healthier bodies and minds. The wheel shape meant that there was no real beginning or end to it, causing the user simply to begin again, but with a new understanding of his or

her life—bringing about healing, teaching, enlightenment and spiritual energy. Significance was attached to the number four—four seasons, four elements, four stages of life, and four wind directions. Four sacred medicines also were used—sweetgrass, tobacco, cedar, and sage—which caused medicine wheels to be divided into four balanced sections. And the four traditional colours used within them were red, yellow, black, and white.

The mixture of traditional and innovative ceremonies within this chapter provides you with a variety of ways of approaching and marking key aspects of your life in the comfort of your own home. *Your Personal Shrine* allows you to recognize the important aspects of your life; *Individual Armour* asks you to think about and artistically depict what you perceive to be your strengths and weaknesses; *Stepping Stones* affords you a chance to celebrate your past, present, and future; and *Medicine Wheel* requires you to use outdoor materials to explore and create a circular representation of your internal world.

Why Ceremonies and Rituals?

Making the items in this chapter will not only give you a chance to honour and appreciate your existence, and bring increased balance and harmony to your life, but it also will promote your artistic abilities.

AIMS

To create a special place where
you can spend time alone
and reflect on life.

MATERIALS

Ornaments, photographs, plants,
personal memorabilia, candles, a
water feature; basic art materials.

Your Personal Shrine

A "shrine" celebrates things that are important in one's life,

so what better place to have one than in your own home?

You may already have areas like a windowsill or shelf on

which you display precious photographs or ornaments, but

the deliberate creation of a site using meaningful

objects can add something special to your life.

1 Think about where you would like your shrine to be as this will dictate its size and probably its nature, too. It's a good idea to seek out a quiet space, away from the main activity of the house.

2 Next, gather together the objects that you may want to include in your shrine. You can incorporate anything you wish, from photographs, ornaments and jewellery, to candles, pebbles and fabrics. Just make sure that all the items have some special meaning for you.

3 Decide whether you are happy to arrange your objects on an existing surface or if you want to make a surface for yourself. If you choose to make one, you could use paper, fabric or cardboard. Perhaps you want to hang something behind it all, create a painted backdrop, or construct a surround for your shrine, too. Feel free to do so using available art materials.

4 Then arrange your objects in whatever way you feel appropriate. You might decide to limit yourself to a particular colour scheme or only use positive things in your life in order to establish a peaceful and pleasant area.

5 If, when completed, your shrine does not make you feel restful, change elements within it until it does: remove some objects so that it is less cluttered, change your central piece, or alter the background colours.

6 Once you are happy with the space you have created, use your shrine as a meditative area. If you want, sit before it every morning, asking it to help you deal with the challenges of your day, and come back to it in the evening with a report of how your day has been. Record in your diary the thoughts and feelings that this brings up.

EXPLORING *your shrine*

It is important for you to consider how you felt about creating this special place that can offer you comfort and act as a sanctuary from your troubles:

▌ Did your feelings about making your shrine change once you actually started gathering and arranging the objects?

▌ What is your overall impression of your finished shrine? What feelings does it stir up in you?

▌ Does it invite you to sit before it and contemplate? If so, how does spending time there feel?

▌ Do you use your shrine often? Why do you think this is?

▌ Do you view your shrine as a permanent fixture in your home?

AIMS

To acknowledge your strengths
and weaknesses—both internal
and external.

MATERIALS

A4 paper and pen; paper, card,
or fabric; scissors; oil pastels,
felt-tip pens or crayons; PVA
glue; collage materials such as
foil, wire, mesh and paperclips.

Individual Armour

Do you have any personal attributes—emotional or physical—

of which you are proud or self-conscious? Or do you feel

uneasy when people praise or criticize you for particular

characteristics? Making armour for yourself gives you a rare

chance to recognize, honour, and protect the whole array of

features that combine to make you the person you are.

1 Take a piece of A4 paper
and write down your
emotional and physical
strengths and weaknesses.
For example, you may like
being empathetic, dislike
being oversensitive, love the
colour of your eyes, but hate
the appearance of your legs.

2 Use this information to
decide the parts of your
body that would most
benefit from armour. For
example, you might want a
card breastplate to depict
your loving qualities but also
to protect your vulnerable

heart. Or, you might want a
mesh helmet that protects
your eyes, while still allowing
you to see out adequately.

3 Gather materials that will
allow you to make your
chosen armour. Make as
many varied pieces as you
want. You might choose to
join them together or leave
them separate. Colour or
glue extra features onto your
armour, if you feel the need.

4 Once it is all completed, put the pieces on and look at yourself in the mirror. Make positive statements about yourself, like, "Your heart is now healing behind this armor." You may wish to write these down in your diary along with any other main emotions that strike you during the process.

EXPLORING *your armour*

Question yourself on why you made the armour you did and what effect it has had on you:

▶ Which areas did you celebrate and which did you protect? If you didn't cover certain areas, was this deliberate? Give reasons.

▶ Why did you select the colours and materials you did to depict certain areas and feelings?

▶ How did you feel when you put on your armour?

AIMS

To celebrate your past, present, and future.

MATERIALS

A4 paper and pen; larger pieces of paper or card; oil pastels or felt-tip pens; scissors; PVA glue; collage materials such as fabric.

Stepping Stones

Rituals like christenings and marriages are celebratory occasions that acknowledge important events in our lives. Creating "stepping stones" symbolic of your past, present and future is an enriching and rewarding activity as it allows you to acknowledge that simple everyday occurrences are just as important in the grand scheme of things.

1 Spend a few minutes thinking about the key elements of your past, present and future. Try to focus on the positive aspects of your life. Write them down on A4 paper and, if you want, draw little pictures to represent them, too.

2 Then take a larger piece of paper or card and use your materials to create a two- or three-dimensional picture that represents a key element in your past. You may, for example, want to illustrate your proudest childhood moment, or you may prefer to think of a more past event. Be free with texture, colour and your imagination.

3 Repeat this to create a second picture but this time concentrate on your current life. This is a celebratory ceremony so identify and honour the positive aspects of the present, even if things are difficult at the moment.

4 Then make a third image to represent your hopes for the future. This is slightly different as it is pure fantasy, and so can be as extravagant and flamboyant as you like.

5 Place your three assemblages of past, present and future across your room like stepping stones on a river. Leave gaps in between so that you can stand in front of each one to get a good view of the next.

6 Walk to and stand in front of your "past stone;" notice or express what you feel about that period; honour it with a positive statement.

7 Do the same for your "present" and "future stones," too, making sure that you always end with a positive statement.

8 Keep a note in your diary of all the feelings that surface, whether positive or negative.

YOU OUTSIDE

EXPLORING *your stepping stones*

This activity can be a very powerful one, at times raising unexpected memories, thoughts and reactions to certain aspects of your life. Be probing yet gentle when questioning yourself on what you have made and why:

▶ Was it easiest to think about your past, or present or future? Why do you think this was?

▶ Did you spend more time making one section than the others? If so, think about why this was the case.

▶ Do you think each of your images is symbolic of that time in your life in general, or does it only represent a very particular moment during that period?

▶ Which of your images did you most enjoy creating? Is it also the one you found most visually pleasing? And is it the one you most enjoyed thinking about when walking? What do you think this reveals about you?

AIMS

To raise your awareness of your
ongoing relationship with nature.

MATERIALS

Natural objects found in a garden
or park; coat hanger; garden
wire; string; scissors; paint and
paintbrushes; PVA glue.

Medicine Wheel

Native Americans used medicine wheels to commune with

nature and to shape the course of their lives. By making one

of your own, you can raise your awareness of nature—its

strengths, energies and importance in your life.

1 Take a walk outdoors and
remove some leaves on their
stalks. Take only from where
there are lots of leaves so
that you merely prune the
plant, rather than destroy it.

2 Also gather feathers, pebbles
and any other natural objects
that have fallen to the
ground. If you do not find
enough material locally, go
further afield. Bring home
and carefully clean
everything you collect.

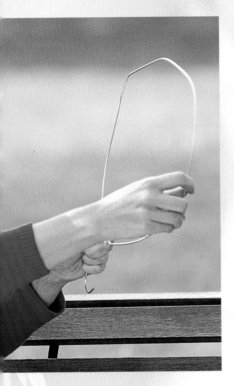

3 Take a wire coat hanger and stretch it into a circular shape. Entwine your leaves carefully around the hanger and attach them securely with garden wire or string.

4 Then use garden wire to divide your circle into four sections, as is traditional when forming a medicine wheel (see pages 108–109 for further explanation).

5 Decorate your circle with the items you have collected. Glue on feathers, or paint objects like pebbles and leaves, and hang these from the rim of your circle with string. You could, for example, paint symbols on four pebbles to represent the four elements. You could introduce red, yellow, black and white—the traditional medicine wheel colours—or you could use colours of your own choice. If you paint pebbles, apply a layer of PVA glue when they are dry to waterproof them.

6 When you have finished, choose a place to hang it up. Record in your diary the feelings that have surfaced during this activity.

EXPLORING *your medicine wheel*

Keep in mind how you felt while making your wheel and compare those feelings with the emotions that the finished piece stirs up:

▶ How did you feel gathering your materials outside? What thoughts did it provoke?

▶ Do you think that working with objects from nature had any impact on your creativity?

▶ How do you feel about your completed medicine wheel?

▶ What revelations about yourself has this activity helped to bring to the surface?

Personal *insights*

PROJECT: Individual Armour

CREATOR: Sara

Sara, a student, wanted to create lightweight
armour that would be easy to wear and
wouldn't restrict her movement in any way.
It was also important to her that it should not
cover too much of her, as she wanted it to
convey protection only, and not concealment.

*The first thing Sara did
was create a cardboard
breatsplate for her heart as she
sees this as the life-giver and
sustainer of the body.*

*She made another plate to
celebrate her womb. The
balloon in the middle would
inflate on attack to provide
extra protection.*

*Sara coloured the plates silver, gold and bronze to
represent the protective qualities of metals, and used
huge paper clips, wire, foil and metal buttons to make
it as much like real armour as possible. She also added
hanging layers of silver card to give the effect of chain
mail. She did not feel, however, the need to cover her
legs, shoulders or arms.*

The other areas Sara wanted to protect were her head and face so she made a helmet to match her body armour in both style and protective qualities. She included the mesh top to double up as a handle for the helmet when it isn't being worn, and she made the elaborate gold visor movable so that it could be lifted up for better vision in times of relative safety.

Sara also wanted strong-looking objects to protect her wrists as they contain powerful pressure points and main arteries. She created them in gold card to convey strength, and gave them jagged edges that she could use to ward people off if necessary.

Exploring Further

It was no surprise to Sara that she decided to make armour for her heart, womb, head and face as she sees these as the four main areas that make up who she is. She realized she chose the heart, as it can be so strong in times of need, yet so sensitive in love— something she has experienced many times. She shielded her womb, as this is where life is created, revealing her desire to have children of her own later on. And her protective headgear guards her knowledge, memories, hopes, fears and desires, as well as covering her face, which she views as her main means of communication with the world. Sara enjoyed wearing her armour as she felt it not only allowed her to protect these four vital areas but allowed her to celebrate and rejoice in them, too.

YOU
in the world

This section is designed to help you realize your significance in

the wider scheme of things and to help put you in touch with

life-enhancing factors out of your direct control, such as the

elements, the seasons and other features of the environment.

Bringing your art outside and interacting with nature will give you

a chance to add a new dimension to your creativity.

The Seasons

The seasons of the year often are seen as reflections of the cyclical nature of life. Taking the seasons as inspiration, and incorporating them into your artistic creations, should help you to understand the constant changes in your life, as well as to appreciate your role in the general scheme of things.

Activities to come

Choosing Your Season

Seasonal Collage

Tribute to the Seasons

Music for all Seasons

Personal *insights*

Tribute to the Seasons

The weather of the four seasons varies widely geographically. Certain countries endure dramatic temperature and climate changes between each one, whereas, in other parts of the world, the seasons merge subtly into one another. But, wherever we live, the changing of the seasons tends to have distinct effects on our well-being and psyche. It is now recognized, for example, that people living in northern countries, which receive less sunlight, can be prone to a reaction appropriately called SAD (Seasonal Affective Disorder). Symptoms of this disorder include sleeplessness, depression and extreme tiredness, and occur mostly in autumn or winter.

The seasons also can affect our moods on a very personal level—each of them having varied effects on different people. For example, you might realize at the end of winter that the first snowdrops of the year entirely lift your mood. Or, a blue sky and sunshine makes you think of summer and feel light-hearted, while rain showers make you feel refreshed and reviatlized. Or, the autumn leaves make you more contemplative than usual. Or, the first snowflakes of winter give you a childish and happy feeling inside.

To think about the cycle of the seasons is to work towards accepting that changes—including both life and death—are to be celebrated, and perhaps even to realize that the search for a clear purpose in

life becomes much less important when we view ourselves as part of something bigger and more significant than our own consciousness.

The activities within this chapter allow you to celebrate the role that the seasons play in your life, and to appreciate the beauty that lies within each of them, whatever your associations with them. *Choosing Your Season* allows you to use the seasons to explore the mood you are in at the time of being creative; *Seasonal Collage* gives you the chance to examine the effect that the current season has on your frame of mind; *Tribute to the Seasons* provides you with an opportunity to consider what your feelings about and memories of each season are in turn; and *Music for all Seasons* combines the rhythmical nature of music with the flowing nature of the seasons to see how they affect and, hopefully, open up your creativity. Enjoy this opportunity to think deeply about the seasons in a way that you don't often do, due to lack of time or motivation.

Why The Seasons?

Working artistically with the seasons can help you to recognize your small but important role in the universe; while using objects from nature in your art can remind you of the importance of respecting nature.

AIMS

To gain a wider understanding
of your own current view
of the world.

MATERIALS

Thick card, tray, or paper plate;
felt-tip pens or paint and
paintbrushes; collage materials
such as shells, cork and other
recyclable objects; PVA glue.

Choosing Your Season

This chance to explore the seasons requires you to think

about your current frame of mind and general attitude to life,

as different seasons are often indicative of different moods.

1 Decide on the season that best matches your current mood, spend a few minutes dwelling on it, and then gather together some materials you feel reflect it.

2 Cut out a piece of thick card in whatever shape you want as a base to work on. Alternatively, you could use an existing item like a tray or paper plate as your base.

3 If you are making a base, decorate it using felt-tip pens or paint. Then arrange available collage materials on it to create a scene that reflects your chosen season, and therefore your current perspective on life. For example, you may decide to capture summer—the season of sun, sea, sand, and fun— by using bright colours, like pink, red and yellow, and incorporating natural objects that you have collected, like shells, sand or flowers.

4 Decide whether you want to glue on your objects or whether you simply want it to be a transient creation.

5 Once you have finished your creation and reflected upon it, feel free to alter it if you think this would help improve your mood. Don't forget to keep a note in your diary of your experiences throughout the activity.

EXPLORING *your creation*

Capturing your current mood in an artistic depiction of one of the seasons can help deepen your understanding of your own frame of mind, so try to learn as much as possible from it:

▶ Which season did you choose and why? Was it restricting to concentrate on only one season?

▶ Did your ideas for the season creation flow easily?

▶ Were you pleased with your creation, or did you choose to alter it? Why was this the case?

▶ Did you want your creation to be permanent or did you destroy it once you had finished? Why do you think this was?

▶ Do you think this activity has helped you have a better understanding of how you are feeling at the moment?

MATERIALS

Found objects from nature;
card; felt-tip pens or paint and
paintbrushes; scissors; collage
materials such as tissue paper
or cord; PVA glue.

Seasonal Collage

Whatever the time of year, you can use it to expand your

creativity, and to explore how in tune you are with nature.

It is important to think about both positive and negative

elements of the present season, which makes this

a good mind-balancing activity.

1 Take a walk outside to look
for natural objects that you
feel reflect the current
season. If you do not have
easy outdoors access,
collect magazine images,
old photographs and other
objects that you have
around the house instead.

2 Think about the colours you
associate with the season, as
well as your feelings about
those particular colours.

for example, use loose leaves and pieces of bark for autumn, or arrange petals to make flowers for spring.

5 Play around with your materials until you are happy with the end result. Then glue your objects in place if you want. The main thing is to enjoy the creation process and to record your thoughts throughout the experience in your diary.

3 With these thoughts fresh in your mind, take a piece of card and decorate it with paint or felt-tip pens to use as a base for your seasonal creation. If you like, cut it into a shape that will help with your interpretation.

4 Start arranging your collected objects on this base to reflect your feelings about the time of year. You might,

EXPLORING *your creation*

Depicting how you feel about the current season can reveal a lot about your present state of mind:

▶ Why did you use the materials you did in your collage? Which features do you prefer and why?

▶ Do you think you gained most from the collection process, the creation process or seeing the end product? What do you think this reveals about you?

▶ Do you view your creation as positive or negative? Do you think it reflects how you feel about the current season?

AIMS

To trace your overall responses
to the four seasons and see
how they affect your life.

MATERIALS

A4 paper and pen; card; felt-tip
pens or paint and paintbrushes;
collage materials such as wire,
thread, cork and fabric.

Tribute to the Seasons

Everyone's moods and energy levels change with the seasons

so it is interesting to think about how your life adapts

as you experience each one. This activity allows you to do

just this by creating artwork that reflects your feelings

on them all, whether combined or individually.

1 Decide whether you would
like to make a separate
creation for each season; to
produce two pieces, one for
negative aspects and one
for positive aspects of the
seasons; or to make just
one creation for all seasons.

2 Once you've decided, think
about and write down on
A4 paper the main ideas that
each season brings to mind.

3 Now choose the type of
creation that you feel can
best illustrate your
thoughts—for example,
a painting, collage or
three-dimensional
construction. Use your
imagination freely to
create a piece that includes
as many of your seasonal
associations as possible.

4 Once you have created your
piece(s) of art, spend a few
minutes looking at it/them
and reflect on what you have
learned from their creation.
Question yourself about your
end product(s) and keep
track of all your findings
and feelings in your diary.

EXPLORING *your images*

Question yourself on your thoughts about the four seasons as they can cause unexpected realizations about yourself and your priorities in life:

▌ Did you choose to create one piece or several pieces of artwork to depict the seasons? Why do you think this was?

▌ Which season did you start with and why do you think this was the case?

▌ Did you identify your favourite and least favourite seasons? How do you adapt your life as you experience each season? What does this reveal about you?

▌ Do you like your finished object(s)? What emotions does your artwork stir in you?

▌ What did you learn about yourself and your attitude to nature by doing this activity?

AIMS

To use music in conjunction
with the seasons as inspiration
for your personal creativity.

MATERIALS

CD or cassette; stereo; large
piece of paper; masking tape;
oil pastels, colouring pencils,
or paint and paintbrushes.

Music for all Seasons

Music is a very powerful medium as it often evokes strong

feelings, associations and memories. This activity gives you a

chance to let music act as an external force affecting

your creativity as well as an emotional stimulant.

1 Select and play a piece of music—it could be a favourite or just whatever is readily available at the time. Listen to the piece and absorb the atmosphere that it creates around you. You may wish to dance and move your body in response to the music. Decide which of the four seasons this piece most reminds you of and why.

2 With the same song playing again, take a large piece of paper, tape its corners to a wall or to the ground, and start transferring your mood, body movements and thoughts from the music onto the paper. Use oil pastels, colouring pencils or paint to express your thoughts and feelings.

3 Think big, free and light, and allow yourself to go with the music's flow and rhythm. If the music stops, simply play it again. Don't analyse the situation as such, just

EXPLORING *your image*

Make the most of this combination of art and music by asking yourself searching questions about the experience:

▶ Did playing music transform your mood and outlook?

▶ Did the music instantly remind you of a certain season? Was it hard to translate this onto paper?

▶ Do you feel that your image truly represented your mood?

▶ Do you feel any different after having done this activity?

enjoy the atmosphere you have created and try to capture it in your creation with your materials.

4 When you have finished your image, stand back and take a long look at it. Which season does it most remind you of, and why? Is it the same season that the piece of music initially brought to mind? Record all your thoughts in your diary.

Personal *insights*

PROJECT: Tribute to the Seasons

CREATOR: Kate

An accountant, Kate decided to create a wire-based model as her tribute to the seasons as she felt that a three-dimensional object for all four seasons could reflect the depth of her passion for nature. She created four separate sections yet tried to make them flow into each other, as the seasons do in reality.

▲ SPRING
First, Kate made little detailed, felt flowers, which implied to her the new growth that comes in spring—life gathering pace again after the winter. She also included a small, green cardboard disc—a colour she sees as most representative of nature in bloom.

▲ SUMMER
Kate saw summer, her favourite season, as the most playful section of her creation. The pink bikini represents Kate's recent increased confidence in her physical appearance that has allowed her to wear a two-piece bathing suit for the first time at the age of 30. The little coloured fish indicate the sea in which she loves to swim. She also included a kite and a rainbow to depict time outdoors, showing how much easier she thinks it is to be active and healthy during the summer months. Another element she added was a cardboard disc the colour of a bright summer sky—a reminder of the kind of day that fills her with happiness.

▼ AUTUMN

Her depiction of autumn evoked strong memories of her childhood–the smell of leaves burning in the neighbourhood, walks in the woods, and wearing rubber boots to rake leaves in the garden. She made a cute, miniature cardboard version of her boots, and used bubblewrap to depict smoke from the fires that she remembered. However, even the smoke looks safe and friendly and isn't interfering with anything or getting in the way–all a very romantic, idealized vignette of her childhood, reminding her how comforting and secure autumn has always felt to her.

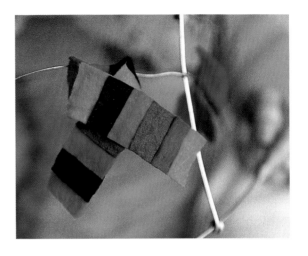

▲ WINTER

Kate views winter as beautiful but harsh, mainly due to the bad weather she has always experienced at this time of the year. The stripey scarf that she made out of felt is a copy of one given to her by her ex-partner to help shield her from the cold. She loves it but unfortunately never wore it until they split up, which causes her some regret. She also included fragile snowflakes, heavy clouds, and a grey disc symbolizing the gloom of winter, alongside an orange one representing the inner fire that keeps her going.

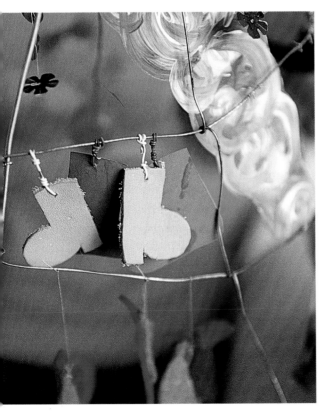

Exploring Further

Kate found her finished tribute to the four seasons very pleasing as it captures and celebrates both positive and potentially negative elements in the seasons, and reflects the cyclical aspects of life. She came to realize through this activity how comforting she finds it to see life as a natural progression of phases, everything changing for a reason, even if that reason is unknown to us for the majority of the time. Considering life like this makes it much easier for her to accept the notions of change and death.

The Elements

Nature's four elements—fire, air, earth and water—are powerful, both as external forces and when internalized. The activities in this chapter enable you to explore and learn from each element, and apply what you learn to boost your creativity, as well as your level of self-comprehension.

It used to be general belief that the world was made up of the four elements—everything had its own unique blend so that each object was slightly different from all the others. Although science has now given us a different interpretation of the world, an insight into the elements and their symbolism still can be useful when considering psychology. Carl Jung used the four elements as a base for his main personality types: sensing (earth), feeling (water), thinking (air) and intuiting (fire). Astrological signs are also divided between the four elements, and each of these—fire, air, earth and water signs—displays some of the traits of its ruling element.

Fire is the traditional source of warmth and comfort, but, when unrestrained, can cause conflagration; air is vital to our existence but too much, in the form of tornados and hurricanes, results in destruction; earth is the source of life, but its earthquakes and volcanos produce death; water makes up seventy per cent of the earth's surface and seventy five per cent of the human body, yet it, too, has its downsides, like tidal waves and floods. Hence there is duality, and indeed variety, to discover within each of the elements.

The elements have inspired many great artists in their work. The music in Beethoven's *Pastoral Symphony* captures everything from the vigour of the storm to the tranquility of a raindrop on a leaf;

and a Debussy composition, entitled *La Mer*, portrays the tumultuous ocean. Shakespeare also used the elements to great effect in many of his works, including *The Tempest*, as even the name suggests. In our time, James Turrell, a land artist, actually uses the earth and sky as his canvas—he has acquired a giant crater in Arizona and is turning it into chambers from which to observe light from the sun, moon and stars.

The activities that follow give you a chance to think about and appreciate the four elements in a way that you probably never have before, and to use them as inspiration for your own creative work. *Choosing Your Element* affords you the opportunity to explore your personal associations with the elements; *Contrasting Elements* enables you to view your own personality in terms of

elemental traits; *Tribute to the Elements* asks you to think about how each element makes you feel; and *Elements and Problem Solving* allows you to identify the positive, reassuring aspects of the elements, and to use them to accept and work through any difficulties in your life.

Why The Elements?

Working creatively in the realm of fire, air, earth and water allows you to discover the huge impact they have on your life. This can help your understanding of yourself, others and the world around you.

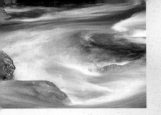

AIMS

To explore your relationship
with the elements and how
they affect your life.

MATERIALS

A4 paper and pen; large
piece of paper; paint and
paintbrushes; collage materials
such as thread, wire, buttons
and sequins; PVA glue.

Choosing Your Element

This activity allows you to spend time thinking about and

appreciating the four elements—fire, air, earth and water—

and deciding which one of them provides you with

the most positive energy for your current mood.

1 Firstly, brainstorm your associations with fire, air, earth and water on A4 paper to help you get to know how you feel about each one. For instance, you might see fire as powerful, threatening and frightening, or you might view it as very warm, cosy and comforting.

2 Now identify the element on which you would most like to focus at the present time. Your decision may reflect your astrological sign, since people born under a certain sign often have a natural affinity with its associated element. For example, people born under a water sign like Pisces or Scorpio may be drawn automatically to water. Or it may be that your mood simply best matches with the features of water at present.

3 Next, try to get into the atmosphere of your chosen element by surrounding yourself with as much of it as possible. For example, if you have chosen water, you could fill a bowl or sink with water, explore the sensation of it running through your fingers as you play with it, and experience its coolness and flowing nature. If your choice was fire, you might sit in front of one, or outside in the sun. Then

close your eyes and absorb the feeling of warmth. For air, you could switch on a fan and let it blow on your face; or for earth, you could take soil from a garden or flowerpot and play around with it in your hands.

4 Once you have done this, think carefully about how you might visually represent the feelings that your element has evoked. Think, for example, about the colours of your element.

5 Using paint, appropriate materials and a large piece of paper, then create an imaginative collage of the element for your mood. Once it is completed, think about why you have made it the way you have. Record your thoughts in your diary.

EXPLORING *your collage*

Creating a collage for the element that most suits your current mood can lead to increased self-comprehension:

▶ Why did you choose the element you did?

▶ What thoughts, feelings or memories did the creative process bring to the surface?

▶ What colours, shapes and objects did you use in your collage? Why do you think you chose to use these?

▶ Does your image accurately reflect how you feel about your chosen element or about your current life in general?

AIMS

To use the elements of nature
to explore opposing sides
of your character.

MATERIALS

A4 paper and pen; large piece of
card; scissors; paint and
paintbrushes; collage materials
such as fabric, sequins; PVA
glue or stapler; tape.

Contrasting Elements

Everyone has various sides to his or her personality.

By looking at how contrasting elements of nature co-exist

within your own character, you can learn how to balance

your positive and negative aspects better and therefore

work towards becoming a more self-assured person.

1 Write down on A4 paper
your main associations with
fire, air, earth and water.
From this, choose the two
elements that you feel
represent your most
dominant character traits.
This activity is most effective
if you choose opposing

elements of yourself, such as fire for your temperamental side and water for the cool, calm and collected you. Then look back at your associations with the two elements you have chosen and develop them further.

2 Gather together collage materials that you feel could depict your associations.

3 Cut your card into whatever shape you want to use as a base, and paint it. Next, arrange, and glue or staple on the collage materials you have collected. You may decide to integrate the two elements or you may want to keep them separate.

4 Once you've formed your image, tape it to the wall and reflect on what is happening in it and how you feel about it. Answer the questions on the right in your diary as a starting point for your personal interpretation.

EXPLORING *your collage*

It can be challenging to think of your own character in terms of elements, so question the process in depth:

▶ Why did you choose the elements you did?

▶ Did you find it hard to create a visual representation of the "elements" in your character?

▶ Was one element more dominant than the other in your collage? Why was this?

▶ Did you feel the finished piece accurately represented you?

▶ Would you like to change your image? If so, how? Does this reflect how you could develop your own character?

AIMS

To celebrate the four elements and realize their importance in your life.

MATERIALS

Large piece of card; scissors; paint and paintbrushes; collage materials such as felt, ribbon and tissue paper; PVA glue.

Tribute to the Elements

Exploring and celebrating the four elements—fire, air, earth and water—and how they affect you on a daily basis will give you an opportunity to look at and acknowledge many aspects of your life, and could help you gain a balanced overview, which, in turn, may be used with future decision-making.

1 Collect materials of varied colours, shapes and textures, which remind you in some way of the four elements— fire, air, earth and water.

2 Decide whether you would like to make one image for all the seasons or four entirely separate images. If you are making one image, cut a piece of card or paper into a circle. This Earth shape can promote the mood of the elements. If you are making separate images, make a different shape to relate to each element.

3 Now paint and decorate each of your card base(s) in any way you want using the collage materials. Focus on one element at a time, so that you give each one your full attention. Use your imagination to make, arrange and stick on any features that you feel will add to your tribute.

4 When you feel your piece is adequately balanced, reflect on what you have created. Record your observations for each element in your diary.

EXPLORING *your creation*

Creating any sort of tribute is a worthwhile process as it allows you to take stock of important aspects of your life that you might otherwise take for granted. Use this tribute to the elements to the full by asking yourself searching questions on the creative experience:

▶ What thoughts and feelings were evoked as you worked your way through each element?

▶ Did you find one element easier to depict than the others or did they all flow easily? Why do you think this was the case?

▶ Was there any imbalance in your representation of the four elements? Did you do this on purpose? What factors might have caused you to do this?

▶ Did you find that certain elements evoked positive associations, while others evoked negative ones? Why do you think this was?

AIMS

To use one of nature's elements
to help you deal with a current
problem or negative emotion.

MATERIALS

A4 paper and pen; large piece of
paper or card; collage materials
such as fabrics, magazines and
photographs; scissors; PVA glue;
felt-tip pens.

Elements and Problem Solving

We all experience negativity from time to time in our lives.

Whatever the problem, this activity gives you the chance

to turn to nature's forces for comfort and reassurance,

in order to work through your problem and try

to create something positive from your situation.

1 Identify the negative emotion that you wish to deal with during this activity.

2 Think about each of the four elements—fire, air, earth and water—in connection with your problem. Jot down your associations on A4 paper.

3 Decide which element might help you most with the issue in hand. Earth, for example, might help you cope with a death, as that person has now become part of the earth and can live again through the plants that spring from it. Or water

may ease the effects of job loss, as water's beauty lies in its constant flux—exactly what this change allows you to have in life. Fire might help you deal with a current sense of apathy or boredom, as it could encourage you to be more passionate and all-embracing; or air could help dispel feelings of loneliness as you imagine the voices of loved ones being carried to you on the wind.

4 Whichever element you choose, think of a way in which you can absorb yourself briefly in it. You

EXPLORING *your creativity*

It can be difficult to associate a negative emotion or experience with one of the elements. However, it is also a very worthwhile process so make sure you question yourself about it:

▶ How did you feel getting closer to "your" element by surrounding yourself in or with it?

▶ What type of product did you make in the end? Why do you think this was?

▶ What colours, shapes and textures did you use and why did you choose each of these?

▶ How effective did you find this whole process? Did it help you put things more into perspective?

could visualize yourself in a suitable environment, like a field, a desert, the seashore or on a hilltop. Alternatively, you might be able to visit somewhere appropriate in person. Otherwise, just make symbolic gestures, such as feeling some earth from a flowerpot, putting your hand in water, lighting a candle or lamp to create fire, or opening the windows to let air circulate more freely. You could take photographs of this if it feels relevant.

5 Next, make a collage or photo-montage based on your feelings about the issue and your chosen element. You might then draw or write on your creation with felt-tips if you want.

6 Try to continue this activity by doing some creative writing, using your artistic creation as inspiration. Record in your diary any strong emotions or realizations that emerge.

Personal *insights*

PROJECT: Contrasting Elements

CREATOR: Nick

A full-time musician, Nick thoroughly enjoyed this opportunity to view his own character in terms of natural elements. He chose fire and water as the two main opposing forces within what he views as his often artistically temperamental personality, and picked red and blue to depict them.

▷ *Nick began by painting a broad band of bright red around the edge of his circle and placed a small circle of blue card in the centre. The red represented his dominant, overly passionate side, while the smaller amount of blue reflected his more relaxed side.*

He attached curved strips of green, blue and silver card over the whole image to create a sweeping sense of movement, like waves. Nick liked these "waves" merging into the "fire," so added some red strips and red sweet wrappers between the sections to give the impression of the elements moving into each other, just as they interact with each other in his character.

To him, his image depicted the whirlwind of emotions he experiences on a daily basis. He therefore made an abstract model of himself by scrunching up and painting masking tape, and placing this in the middle. He then scattered tangled blue and red thread over it and the rest of the creation to show his current uncertainties about himself and life.

Exploring Further

Nick was proud of his finished creation as he felt that it reflected the mood swings and imbalances in his character that he has been trying to address recently. He felt stronger for having transferred the problems, which previously existed only in his head, onto paper. This gave him a sense of being more in control of his own life. He would like to throw away his creation in order to symbolize letting go of his formerly moody and often angry self, and letting his calmer, more balanced persona take the lead.

PROJECT: Choosing Your Element

CREATOR: Emma

A primary school teacher, Emma chose water as the element most representative of her mood at the time of this activity. She felt water was appropriate for her because of its dual aspect— an appearance of calm on the surface, yet capable of a lot of passion, energy and excitement when stirred up in any way.

Emma glued some rectangles of card in a range of blue-green shades onto white paper, only slightly overlapping them. She saw these coloured patches of card, along with the green and blue paint that she splattered across the image, as an attempt to capture the diversity of water, and in particular the ocean. The brighter blues and greens show a calm, safe, inviting sea, while the muddy greens depict the ever-present possibility of pollution and danger.

She felt that she included the specks of silver paint, the little beads, and the pearls, pasta shells, and glitter, to represent the beauty and treasures that can be found in the sea. The pieces of broken, coloured glass, on the other hand, show, to her mind, that what is beautiful can also be deadly if not looked after and respected.

Exploring Further

Emma really enjoyed depicting water as it encompasses so many aspects of life that she enjoys: fun, excitement, beauty, and great variety; but also a sense of danger and the unknown. She was delighted with her finished collage, not only because she finds it attractive and reassuring to view, as with the real ocean, but also because she came to see it as an effective metaphor for life— strong, mysterious, and in constant flux. She thinks her image a very positive one, which reflects her good mood at the time of its creation. Emma really appreciated this activity as it gave her the chance to realize just how confident she was feeling.

Environment

Landscapes and the plants and animals that inhabit them contain a lot from which we can learn. The activities in this chapter will help to heighten your awareness of the natural world around you, and encourage you to celebrate and appreciate its many aspects at every opportunity.

The ancient Greeks worshipped the Earth goddess Gaia, and believed that her territory, the Earth, was to be protected and valued. Those who took good care of it were believed to be rewarded with abundant harvests and flourishing livestock; while those who abused it were thought to be punished with famine and disease. Imagine the punishment we would be receiving today from Gaia with the pollution that we currently create! We seem to be taking the natural beauty of our world for granted, rather than respecting and learning from it. It is important that each one of us takes notice of and some responsibility for the environment that surrounds us and makes our lives what they are.

Nature and the environment have inspired artists for millenia. Aboriginal art, for example, has always been environmentally-based: a traditional artistic technique was engraving images on the bark of Eucalyptus trees. Many painters, too, including the French Impressionists, based their work on aspects of the environment, such as Claude Monet's *Waterlilies*. When Monet started to work outdoors on natural subjects, he described it as having a veil torn away, opening up for him his destiny as a painter. Many of his creations aimed to capture the interplay between light, atmosphere, and another object, such as water.

Other artists have been inspired by preservation of the environment, hence what is known as Earthworks or Land Art. Andy Goldsworthy, for example, works with twigs, leaves, stones, snow, and ice, to try to discover more about nature's wonders. He sees the transience of his creations as crucial in order to reflect the ever-changing environment in which we live; Richard Long makes geometric sculptures using found objects, with a particular interest in the significance of stones and rocks, in order to respond to the "real" influences that he sees around him; and Robert Smithson's *Spiral Jetty* (1970), a gigantic spiral made out of rocks and earth on the shores of Utah's Great Salt Lake, is one of his many works in land, rather than on land, which aim to bring together people and nature.

This chapter urges you to follow in the footsteps of such artists. *On the Beach* allows you to make transient creations outdoors; *Natural Sculpture* asks you to create a piece in keeping with your surrounding environment; and *Animal Activity* lets you explore your own attitudes to wildlife.

Why Environment?

Taking objects in the landscape, or plants and animals, as inspiration for your creativity urges you not only to appreciate the beauty and importance of nature, but also to consider how it affects your daily life.

AIMS

To use the beach as your creative inspiration in order to come to terms with the notion of impermanence.

MATERIALS

Beach location; found objects from the beach; bucket and spade; camera.

On the Beach

This activity will enable you to feel free, to work on a scale which is impossible at home, and to enjoy yourself in the way children do when they visit the seashore. It will help you to appreciate that you can't always keep what you have created, and will teach you to let go of the grasping side of your character that always likes to feel in control.

1 On arrival at the beach, spend some time just walking around, getting into the feel and mood of it. Take off your shoes, feel the sand beneath your feet, and paddle in the water.

2 Then survey your surroundings, and select a suitable place for you to work creatively.

3 Next, take a walk up the beach, looking for objects like pebbles, shells, driftwood, and seaweed to use for your beach creation.

4 Go back to your selected area and begin making a "sculpture" with the objects you have collected. You could use your bucket and spade to build a sand sculpture and adorn it with your found objects, or you may prefer to make a more abstract work.

5 Take as much time as you want arranging and rearranging your sculpture, bearing in mind that you are at the mercy of the tide!

6 You may wish to take photographs of your creation when you have finished so that you have a lasting souvenir of it. Then contemplate how the whole process has affected you. Record in your diary any observations you make or feelings you experience.

Making something temporary outside is a very different artistic experience so question yourself on how it has affected you:

▶ How did it feel to be out in the open, exposed to other people? Did you gradually forget where you were working?

▶ Why do you think you made the creation you did in the end?

▶ Did you feel a need for other people's reactions or approval?

▶ How did you feel, knowing that your creation would be swept away by the tide?

AIMS

To explore your connection
with nature in a nearby
outdoors environment.

MATERIALS

Plastic bag; greenery and objects
found outside; garden cane, wire,
or string; camera.

Natural Sculpture

When out in nature, we often feel a need to preserve the moment—to enjoy the freedom and fresh air by smelling the flowers or freshly-cut grass, touching the bark of a tree, making a daisy-chain, or running through a pile of autumn leaves. Your sculpture is simply another way of celebrating this richness of nature.

1 Take a walk somewhere outdoors, like your garden, a local park, or in a field. Gather up in a bag any of nature's fallen treasures that catch your attention, such as feathers, pebbles and stones, twigs, leaves, berries or dead flowers. Don't pick things that are growing as you don't want to harm the natural surroundings.

2 Once you have collected these "accessories," find a clearing or space in which you are happy to create a sculpture with them.

3 Assemble your objects in any way you wish, using garden cane or wire to hold them together, if you like. Otherwise, be inventive!

4 Try and create something that blends in with the environment you are in, rather than making too obvious a statement.

5 Once you have created your sculpture, you may wish to take photographs of it as a souvenir. Then sit before it, thinking about the activity you have just engaged in, and absorb your creativity.

6 You can, if you like, take your creation apart before leaving, or simply allow it to disintegrate naturally. Keep a note of any observations you made or insights you gained in your diary.

EXPLORING *your sculpture*

Working with items from nature outdoors might greatly impact on your creativity so consider how different this is to when you work artistically with man-made materials indoors:

▶ How did you find the process of creating spontaneously in this way? How did you feel about being outdoors? Did you feel self-conscious and intimidated by passers-by, or did you feel entirely free?

▶ Did you have a preconceived idea of how you wanted your sculpture to look or did you simply let it grow?

▶ What do you think your natural sculpture reveals about you and your view of the world?

▶ How did you feel about the end product? Were you very critical about it? Were you happy with it? Did you feel that, given more time, you could have done a better job? Was it hard to leave your sculpture behind?

MATERIALS

A4 paper and pen; large pieces
of paper or card; felt-tip pens or
paint and paintbrushes; fabrics;
PVA glue; collage materials such
as tissue paper and feathers.

Animal Activity

We have a lot to learn from nature and wildlife. The following

activity enables you to choose the animal you would most

like to be, and get "under its skin" in order to explore what it

is about it that most appeals to you. This process may

help you to discover a lot about your own character

as well as your views on animals.

1 Think about animals generally until you decide with which one you can identify most. Then spend a few minutes writing down on A4 paper the features and characteristics you associate with that animal, and what in it most captures your attention and interest.

2 Now gather together materials that you associate with it to create a collage, painting, mask or costume that attempts to reflect these characteristics. It might be paper, fabrics, paints or feathers—anything appropriate that you have around the house. You are not required to make an image of an actual animal, just to try and capture the essence of your animal with patterns, colour and texture.

3 Once you have finished making your creation, pin up your artwork, lay out your collage or put on your costume. Look at your image on the wall or costume in the mirror and decide if you think it's effective.

4 If you've made a mask or costume, try making the sounds of the animal and moving like it to get into character. Try not to worry about feeling silly as you do this—just enjoy the chance to let go of your inhibitions.

5 Keep track in your diary of the thoughts and feelings that arose as you tried to capture the essence of, and empathize with, the animal you had chosen. Record the main effects you think this activity has had on you.

EXPLORING *your creation*

This activity can cause unexpected realizations about your own views so make sure you question yourself on it:

▶ Why did you choose the animal you did?

▶ Why do you think you made the associations you did with your chosen animal?

▶ Do you think your artistic creation captured the essence of your animal?

▶ If you made a mask or costume, were you able to get into the role of your animal?

▶ Did your feelings about animals change as a result of doing this activity?

Personal *insights*

PROJECT: Animal Activity

CREATOR: Samantha

This activity allowed Samantha, who has a strong interest in psychology, to think about her some of her favourite animals. She realized that she most identifies with cats and aspires to be like them in some ways. She therefore decided to make a feline-inspired costume.

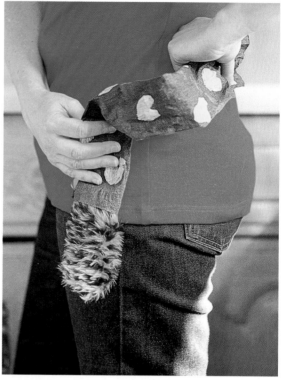

Samantha made a cat costume—tail, claws, furry arm covers and a large face mask with a mane. She felt that this would allow her to acknowledge the feline elements that live within her, and also to adopt the strong, sophisticated characteristics of the feline family that she holds in such high regard.

She feels that she shares a childish, playful quality with the cat family and therefore made a fun, spotted tail for herself, with a furry end. Wearing and waggling this helped her get more into character.

She then made claws to depict a cat's strong sense of family protection and affection, also important elements in her life. She felt that these claws could be used to ward off "enemies," but also to play with friends.

Samantha loves cats' soft fur and deep eyes so full of expression, and so made arm covers and a mask to adorn herself with these attractive features. She felt very liberated in her costume, and was able to adopt the relaxed, elegant, feline attitude that she admires and aspires to have in her daily life.

Exploring Further

Samantha really enjoyed making her costume as she loves animals but doesn't often have the chance to consider them in depth. Thinking about them transported her to her childhood when she was surrounded by animals—a cat, a dog, rabbits and chickens, as well as turtles and fish. She realized that her favourite animals have always been the ones she can pet as she finds it relaxing to stroke them. Samantha recalled the adorable, playful, white kitten that she was given when she was 11 years old. For Samantha, this activity was really rewarding and enriching as it led her not only on a trip down memory lane, but also on a trip of self discovery about her own character and views.

Progressing Forward

The creative projects within this book are likely to have led you to have all sorts of artistic experiences and personal discoveries. It is now important to recognize and celebrate what you have achieved, and think about what steps you might want to take next.

The chapters in *You inside* gave you an initial chance to explore your inner self. *The Scribble* and *Mind and Body* projects guided you in breaking away from preconceived ideas into a rich vista of creative freedom; *Working with Clay* encouraged messiness in your creativity; and *Your Dreams and Senses* helped to develop your powers of appreciation and imagination.

You outside then built on these experiences. *Mask-making* urged you to consider how you present yourself to others; *Assemblages* allowed you to turn odds and ends into meaningful finished pieces; and *Ceremonies and Rituals* led you to find new ways of honouring your past, present and future.

Finally, *You in the world* provided you with a chance to make many connections with nature. Your exploration of the *Seasons*, *Elements*, and *Environment* encouraged you to appreciate, celebrate and respect nature and your small but significant role within it.

You will have acquired many souvenirs along the way—both in terms of physical artwork and lasting emotions. It is important to survey these gifts and decide what you are going to do with them, and whether you plan to continue the creative quest you have now started.

Once you have questioned yourself in depth about your end pieces, it's time to make

a choice: are you going to keep them? What you decide to do with your artwork depends on what exactly you have made, and how you feel about them. You could tuck them in a cupboard for future reference, mount an exhibition or display them on the mantelpiece to be admired, give them away to friends and family, or actually use or wear them from time to time to get the most out of them? Do whatever is best for you with each individual piece.

It is also important to think about how to continue your exploratory, creative journey. It is helpful to repeat the activities at various times as you get very different results depending on your mood. Having done this, you could invite friends around to do the activities together, or join an art course based on the artistic preferences you have discovered during the activities. If you feel that your experiences have unearthed emotions that you need to explore further, consider seeing a professional art therapist, or seeking counselling. There is a wide

choice of types of therapy, from dance and drama therapy, to colour therapy.

Above all, be sure to make a commitment to free up space and time to honour and appreciate yourself. And remember that this has been just the beginning of a new chapter in your life enriched with creative adventure, awareness and fulfilment.

Index

Acknowledgements

Firstly, I would like to thank Jean Campbell, my dear friend and mentor, for her unstinting support, inspiration and ideas throughout the birth and conception of this book. Next, I owe a special thank you to Assia Khashoggi, a model student and my personal assistant, for giving so generously of her time and creative energies. Thanks, too, to my close friends Eileen Bellot and Chris Davis, who have accompanied me on my art therapy journey for many years and are themselves fearless creators.

I express my thanks to my City University students, many of whom will go on to make wonderful art therapists, for their unceasing creative energy—especially the very talented Jessica Collier. Thanks to Takana Tanaka, Sachi Matsubara, Amy Poole, Nadia Swalens, Ceri Passmore, Suzanne Cohen, Josephine Hogg, Katie Baddams and Kath Stanton. Many thanks also to Brenda Louisy, Jonny Lynch and Glen Morrison from Lambo Day Centre. I deeply appreciate my many friends who were generous with their time and energy: a big thank you to Rudolfo Perez, Michele Munnelly, Marilyn Figueira, Karl Theobald, Sasha Lowther, Cherry Lawrence, Ann Hanson, Karim Chibah, Anne Chibah, Andy Shone, Nahia San Pedro, Den Cox, Catherine Magnani, Muriel Hudson, Angela Swalens, Joan Tires, Rachel Roberts and Ailsa Yexley. And I want to express my gratitude to Jack Massarik for his literary support and encouragement.

Last but not least, thanks to the wonderful team who excelled in their own creativity bringing such an aesthetically pleasing book together—particularly Kelly Thompson for her editing expertise and the unique sensitivity that she projected throughout the project, Emily Cook for her wonderful creative direction, and Jules Selmes for his inspiring photography.

USEFUL ADDRESSES

Vicky Barber, art therapist and author
website: www.vickyb.demon.co.uk

British Association of Art Therapists
5 Tavistock Place, London, W1H 9SN
website: www.baat.org